A PARISH
CATECHUMENATE

A PARISH

Catechumenate

Materials and Format for Adult Catechesis

by

JOSEPH V. GALLAGHER, C.S.P.

Director, Paulist Institute
for Religious Research

NEWMAN PRESS

Westminster, Md.   New York, N. Y.   Glen Rock, N. J.

Amsterdam   Toronto

NIHIL OBSTAT: Reverend Robert E. Hunt, S.T.D.
            Censor Librorum

IMPRIMATUR: Most Reverend Thomas A. Boland, S.T.D.
            Archiepiscopus Novarcensis

December 30, 1966

Library of Congress
Catalog Card Number: 67-18461

Jacket Design: Emil Antonucci

Published by Newman Press
Editorial Office: 304 W. 58th St., N. Y., N. Y.   10019
Business Office: Westminster, Md.   21157

Manufactured in the
United States of America.

Contents

Part I

A Presentation of the Gospel

Part II

A Preparation for Baptism

FOREWORD

Catechetical renewal has progressed to the point where poverty pockets are painfully noticeable. One of these areas of lag is in "adult" catechesis, a sector of religious education that has barely begun to profit from the best developments and insights of contemporary catechetics. Substantial efforts have been made in some places to break away from the old inquiry class with its concentration on doctrine and apologetics. In many parishes around the country real innovations have been made both as to format and content, and these promise to develop into new and valuable structures of the apostolate. However, relatively few people are acquainted with these experiments and there is very little in print available to the priests and laity who are engaged in the formation of adults for life in the Church. In this busy apostolate, the pioneers have little time to arrange their material and experience for publication. Too many things are changing too fast.

Yet the need for new material is great. Because of this, the Paulist Institute for Religious Research presents here one such program that incorporates elements of current catechetics, liturgy, ecumenics and scripture. Doubtless there are other programs that have proved their worth in the arena of parish experience. The one here presented was tested in the Diocese of Richmond in a half-dozen parishes over a period of one year with good results. The lessons learned in that experiment have been incorporated here. In the belief that this program will be of interest and aid to many parishes and information centers during this time of transition, the Paulist Institute has assembled the material and format used in this experiment and offers it as one example of a parish catechumenate.

I am indebted to many persons for the material in this book. My brother Paulists of the faculty and student body at St. Paul's College, Washington, D.C., composed the liturgy and homilies that lie at the heart of this catechesis. Those priests of the Diocese of

1

Richmond and their wonderful lay catechists, who piloted this program in their parishes, translated an idea into a reality. Without the help of all these and many others who contributed advice and suggestions, this book could never have been written.

JOSEPH V. GALLAGHER, C.S.P.
Director, Paulist Institute
for Religious Research

Elements of a Parish Catechumenate

Pastoral renewal today is centered in the parish. Whatever may be the future place of the parish in the Church, today it remains true that the parish is the principal point of departure for pastoral work. Consequently, in structuring convert catechesis, our objective is some kind of parish catechumenate.

The word 'catechumenate' is used both because this institution has a long and honored history in the Church, and also because it is broad enough to include several subsidiary structures like the inquiry class, liturgical formation programs, discussion groups, etc., all of which play a contributory role in the formation of a Christian.

This Christian formation is the goal of all catechesis. It is not enough to instruct a person in the truths of faith. The life of God's People demands more. The Christian is called to throw himself fully into the life of God and engage his whole being in the joyful freedom of the divine way of life. To do this requires as much formation as information. It requires prayer and the experience of God's presence in the eucharist and in the Christian community. It requires interchange with other Christians. In short, it requires an introductory experience of the mystery of Christ in his Church.

To house and order these elements is the function of the catechumenate. What they are and where they belong are determined by the facts of Christian life. Liturgy and Laity are not added to an instruction program simply because people expect this kind of thing today. They are there because they provide adequate answers to definite needs in Christian formation. The rationale of the catechumenate program that follows is based upon the multiple needs of those who come to the Church. If one approach could satisfy all of them adequately, there would be no point to this program. But experience teaches us that the grace of Christian vocation causes a far-reaching change in the life of a human being. This change does not take place all at once but is gradual and marked by fairly well-defined stages. Thus, a man must first become interested in the Church before he will give serious attention to her message. Then, he must listen to what she has to say and come to some decision about it. Finally, if he believes and wants to become part of the Church, he must be prepared for the Christian life.

It is both the glory and the weakness of the old inquiry class that it tried to satisfy all of these needs by itself. In the nature of things, it could not do so adequately. At each of these stages, the particular needs of a person are somewhat different and must be met by successive and distinct approaches. The Church must first claim a person's attention. She must then give an account of herself. When this is accepted, she must then go on to introduce the new disciple into her way of life. It is to meet these needs as they occur that there are different programs, each with its distinct content and format, in this catechumenate.

We shall present the catechetical material for each of these stages in their chronological order.

We begin by simply taking note of the first phase, *i.e.,* interest in the Church. No special material for this phase is included here.

Getting Interested in the Church

This first stage can be disposed of very briefly. It may or may not involve a conscious decision or even a religious act. However, it is at least a necessary pre-condition, if not a sign, of Christian vocation. Before a person can confront Christ in the Church, he must give his attention to the Church. This supposes enough interest on his part to lead him to look into the matter. If this interest is not aroused through the manifold circumstances of his life through which God presumably is constantly speaking to him, then the Church must actively aim at stimulating such an interest and thus gain his attention.

Catechists call this activity of the Church pre-evangelization because, in the nature of things, it must precede the preaching of the Gospel. Beyond describing it, and showing how it fits into the mission of a parish, this program does not deal with this aspect. The reason is that there is no special vehicle for pre-evangelization. We must deal with people where they are, and few people stand at the same threshold of interest. The people who come to us are already interested; the others may or may not respond to particular approaches. Personal conversation is the only sure way to discover what interests a man about the Church.

However, there are many existing features of parish life that by their very nature incline to meet this need. The worship life of the parish, its liturgy and piety, the apostolic quality of its members, their involvement in works of social and civic significance, its vitality and style—all of the things we group under the term 'witness,' are potential attention-getters.

Moreover, there are particular parish activities that can develop interest in the Church in more direct fashion. Thus, the traditional inquiry class or lecture series on the Church, a parish forum on matters of Christian interest, discussion club programs, book clubs, etc., are valuable suppliers of truth about the Church that can quickly enlarge the interest and understanding of the casual inquirer and help him toward the next stage in his journey. For this reason, existing programs of this kind should not be discarded until a parish is satisfied that their function is taken up by something else.

There is much to recommend the practice of spending the first couple of sessions of a parish catechumenate in a general discussion of religion, God, the Church, etc. These can provide a helpful bridge from the life of the catechumen into the mystery of the Church that now confronts him. The religious background of the catechumens is the most important factor in making such a decision. Generally, if the group has a good Christian background, some things can be taken for granted. If the group is largely non-church in background, then it might be wise to prepare them for the Gospel by some basic discussion about religion in general. The first lesson in the presentation of the Christian faith that follows does this in summary fashion.

Once a stable interest in the Church is reasonably assured, the task is to present the essentials of Christianity as they are understood and lived by the Catholic Church. This is the second element of the parish catechumenate.

Hearing the Christian Message

The basic Christian message is the good news that God has entered the life of man in a saving action. When a person is ready to listen to the Church, this is the first thing he should hear. So, the next phase of the catechumenate consists in preaching the Gospel.

The material that follows covers the history of salvation in seventeen installments. It is heavily scriptural and calls for the actual reading of scripture in each session. Its purpose is to convert the hearer to Christ. To accomplish this, it relies principally upon the power of the Word of God and the witness of the Christians engaged in the program. For this reason, it is very important that some lay people as well as a priest participate in the program. The task of the lay catechist in this part of the catechumenate is principally to lead discussion at the end of each session. The discussion questions are designed to relate the material of salvation history to the group. For this reason, the discussion part of the program is as important as the presentation.

There is little detailed moral teaching in these lessons, and nothing of Church discipline. These are reserved for the next phase when those who have decided to enter the Church are prepared for Catholic life.

This part of the catechumenate can be open to everybody insofar as numbers allow. It should not be advertised as an inquiry class or a course in the Catholic religion. This is not what it is. It is rather a presentation of the essence of Christianity as experienced by the Catholic Church. It is as much a preaching as a teaching, and its religious nature should be conveyed in the announcements about the program.

Where numbers are small, several neighboring parishes could combine and present a single series, with priests and laity of all the participating parishes contributing to the program.

The presentations are not all exactly the same length, but they are intended to take about 45-60 minutes. Time should be allowed for a discussion period of about 30-40 minutes. A coffee break between is recommended.

None of the material is meant to be followed slavishly. It is presented only as a sample of the type of presentation that incorporates modern catechetical developments. The instructor is expected to bring his own faith, understanding, and personality to bear upon the presentation for he is as much a witness as a teacher.

Part I
A Presentation of the Gospel

GOD'S CHURCH AND MAN'S FAITH

Note: If a catechumenate program includes preliminary dis-cussions about the Church, religion, purpose of life, etc., this lesson should be omitted and the presentation of the "good news" begun with the one following. Otherwise, this can be used for the opening session.

Good evening, and welcome to our series in the Catholic religion. During the next few months we will explore together the things that Catholics believe, the way in which they worship, and everything that goes with 'being Catholic.' At the end of these sessions you will have a pretty good understanding and apprecia-tion of the Catholic Church. For those of you who are believing Christians, I promise that whatever you learn here can help you be better Christians. But whatever your belief, I am sure that all of you will learn something that will help in some way. And if I succeed in giving you this much, I shall count my time well spent.

A word about our procedure: If during this course it seems that I am taking the long way around in explaining things, please be patient. The Catholic religion is a whole that must be described from different angles. We must start piece by piece, and if it doesn't make very much sense for awhile, don't think that you are stupid. Give it some time and the pieces should begin to fall into place and some kind of understandable picture begin to emerge. Naturally, you will have questions. Many of them will be answered in the course of time. If you have others that don't seem to be taken up, feel free to ask about them. That is what we are here for.

Personal Decision

Studying religion is unlike studying anything else. After all, it doesn't make a whole lot of difference to you personally if two

9

and two make four or if they don't. Life goes on in either case. But in religion you are dealing with the most important and most personal facts of life: God, and man's relation to him, human purpose and ideals, man's vision of the world and his future. These matters certainly affect us personally, so there is a very personal stake in the study of religion that is not present in the study of other subjects. It can, and often does, change a person's life.

Some of you may be apprehensive about this. You may worry that I will try to convert you, and you may not want to be converted. Let me assure you at the outset that only God can convert you, and even he won't do it without your consent. If you don't want to become a Catholic, don't worry, you won't. I could not in conscience receive you into the Church unless you really were convinced that this is where you belong. If God wants to convert you that is between you and him. My job is simply to show you the Catholic faith. What you do with it after that is out of my control. However, let me say that as a Catholic, I believe that all of the things that I say to you are true, and I also believe that they can be seen as true by others, and that when a person comes to see the Catholic Church for what she really is, he will want to become a Catholic. So, in this sense, exposure to the Catholic faith can move a person to conversion. This may happen to some of you here and, God willing, I hope that it does. But if it does, it won't be because of me and my explanations or arguments. It will be because God shows something to you that you didn't see before.

Learning from Prayer and Worship

Because of this religious nature of our course, and because some of you have probably come here to discover whether the Catholic Church has anything to offer you, I strongly urge that you make prayer a regular part of these weeks. Ask God to help you gain from them whatever he thinks best for you and leave it to him to decide what that should be. In line with this, starting next week we will begin each evening with a prayer to the Holy Spirit for guidance. I hope that you will all join in, but if there is anyone who prefers not to, naturally we will respect his wishes.

Finally, Catholic life is not simply a matter of believing. It is also doing, and this is every bit as important as believing. I can describe a lot of what we believe, but if you want a sample of Catholic 'doing,' I would urge you to go to Sunday Mass during these weeks. There, you will experience in a way that I cannot convey in class what it means to be a Catholic. Catholics are nowhere more Catholic than at worship. The same, of course, is true of Protestants. So, if you want a lesson in the Catholic faith that I could never give in the classroom, try going to Mass. One of the co-instructors will be glad to help you by explaining the Mass and showing you how to follow along with a prayerbook.

So much for the course itself. Now let me tell you a little bit about the subject matter. Our subject is religion. The Christian religion in particular, and specifically the Catholic Church.

The Christian Religion

Religion can be described as the sum total of man's relations with God. This means that religion involves all those things that tie God and man together, things like faith, prayer, worship, morality, etc. God's actions and man's actions. Religion deals with facts about what God and men have done in the past, are doing now, and can be expected to do in the future. Religion involves all men, even atheists, because all men are related to God whether they know it or not. All of the religions of the world, past and present, deal with these basic things. Some religions are very simple, others are more complicated and have detailed beliefs and practices. The differences among religions are mainly caused by men's different understanding of their position in the universe and their notion of God. We are not going to concern ourselves, except incidentally, with religions other than the Christian religion, for that is what the Catholic Church is and that is what you came to learn about.

The big difference between the Christian religion and all others is that Christians, both Catholic and Protestant, believe that all of their relationship with God is tied up with Jesus Christ. Right away this sets us off from other religions because, as Christians, we cannot talk about God or our relation to him without talking about Christ. In Christ, we discover all that we mean to God and all that God means to us, all that we have to give to God and all that God gives to us. In other words, the Christian religion is not a religion that man has worked out by meditating on his observation and experience. It comes rather from what God has done and what he has shown us about himself and his relationship to us. We believe that he has done this completely in Jesus Christ, and so we look to Jesus for our religion and find there all that we need.

The heart of the Christian religion is the 'good news,' or 'gospel,' that God has entered into the life of man in such a way as to transform it, taking away its limitations and failures in order that man may enter the life of God and find his happiness there forever. To see how God did this and what it means to man, the Christian looks at Christ and there discovers all the truth about God and man.

Catholics and Other Christians

We Catholics believe that the Catholic Church and the Christian religion are inseparable. Even though over the years, various misunderstandings and divisions have grown up between Christians, we believe that the Catholic Church is still the same collection of believers that was formed around Christ, still believing the same things he taught, and still held together by the same bonds of love and obedience toward him. We believe that Christ is still with us in this Church and that it is through the Church that man meets God and faces up to what God expects of him, and either accepts or rejects him. For those who accept him, the Church becomes the home where man lives out his life with God in this world. As for those Christians who are not Catholics, we believe that they, too, are somehow part of the Church, even though they do not live their life with God in the very same way as Catholics and do not participate in every phase of Catholic life. We know that this separation is un-Christian. We know that Jesus wants all Christians to live the one Christian life together. But things have happened that can't be undone. We are grateful that today so many Christians of every church are trying to remedy this. Real progress in unity is being made and, with God's help, we look forward to the time when all Christians will find the full unity of Christ.

What Is Faith?

You will be hearing a lot about faith and it might be well to say a word about this now. In religion, we must never forget that we are involved with God, and this means that in religion things are different in many ways from the rest of our experience. Not contradictory, but different. In dealing with God we don't do so as equals, for we can never be equal to him. He is far more than the best that man can be. We are dependent upon him like children upon a parent, but like a parent, he knows and loves us before we know and come to love him. When a man meets God, it is only because God has first put himself in man's path. He speaks to man and reveals himself in different ways. You will be hearing how he did this in the past and how he does it in the present.

Man's reaction to God is faith. Faith is a very rich experience as we will try to show. It is man's response with all that he has,—mind, heart, and emotion—to the God who comes personally to him in Christ.

There are many things about God we cannot fully understand since our minds are limited and God isn't. But we can trust him, because he has shown that he is good and that he never goes back on his word. God has taught us many things over the centuries and promised us much. Part of faith is man's acceptance of what God has said. Coming to know him is all that is necessary. Once we know him we not only want to belong to him, but we also know we can trust him and believe all that he tells us. When a man 'believes' something he means that he accepts it as true, not necessarily because he sees it, but because he knows the person who tells him this thing, and from what he knows about this person, he knows he can rely on his word. So, in faith we may not see why or how something is so, but we believe it because we do see that God is behind it, and once we know that, it is enough. God can't be wrong and he won't fool us.

In talking about the Catholic faith, then, we don't start in midair. We have something to go on, namely God's words and deeds. That's why we believe that truth is accessible in religion as in other things. We believe that God has a definite plan for man; that there is a definite relationship between God and man; that God has acted and spoken to us about his plan; that he expects us to do something about it. We believe all of these things on the strength of what Jesus Christ has said and done. This is the Catholic religion and these are the things we will be talking about.

But before we come to Jesus Christ, we have to go far back into history and see where Jesus came from. God began to build up the Christian religion a long time ago and to understand it, we must retrace his steps and see how men came to believe. This is how it happened not only for these men long ago, but this is pretty much how it happens still to everyone who comes to believe in Jesus Christ.

Questions for Discussion

What is religion?
Is religion for everybody?
How does a person look for God?
What is special about Christianity?
What is the main point of the Catholic Church?
What does it mean to 'believe'?
How can believing God change a person?

Basic Bibliography

The Point of Catholicism, Cecily Hastings (Sheed & Ward Canterbury Books)
What Is Faith? Joseph Cahill, S.J. (Paulist Press Doctrinal Pamphlet Series)

GOD COMES TO MAN

God has a definite plan for man. It involves all of us and each person has a special part to play in it. As Christians, we know what the plan is: God in his generosity wants to share what he has with us, viz., his life of perfect and uninterrupted happiness. God put his plan into action a long time ago. It took time for men to learn the plan, not because God could not explain it, but because men were more interested in plans of their own.

However, God has unlimited patience and he kept after men until he succeeded in convincing some of them that what he was offering was not only desirable but possible. He had so much respect for man's freedom, however, that he would not force himself on anyone. Rather, he depended upon patient repetition to attract man's attention and gain a hearing. What he wanted from man was simply his free acceptance and cooperation in the plan. When he got this, he could begin to work with man to bring about what he promised. The history of God's approach to man is found in the early part of the Old Testament and we will follow the main steps through which that plan has become known to us.

God made a start with a man named Abram. This man lived in what is now Iraq about the year 1850 B.C. He was a herdsman who lived a nomadic existence with his flocks of sheep, goats and camels. Like most people of that time, he was probably a pagan in religion. This means that he had only a confused notion of God. He probably thought that there were a lot of gods. Why God picked him, we don't know. All we know is that God came to him in some way and made him an invitation.

• READING FROM GEN. 12:1-8.

The meeting between Abram and Yahweh is the first step we know of in the establishment of God's plan in the world. (Yahweh is the Hebrew name for God and we will use it during this part of the course because this is what he is called in the Old Testament. No one is quite sure of the exact meaning of the word, but it means something like 'he who is.') The exchange that takes place between Yahweh and Abram is not very complicated and few details are given. Yet, this encounter is momentous, for it opens a new era in the relations between God and man in the world. Basically, it involves an invitation and a promise. If Abram will leave his homeland and follow Yahweh's lead he will receive a land of his own and become the father of a great nation. He will also receive blessings and protection from Yahweh, and through him all the rest of men will also be blessed.

Abram probably didn't understand what all this meant, but he knew about land and nations. Enough of Yahweh's power and majesty was impressed upon him by this experience so that he 'believed the Lord' (Gen. 15:6), and obediently left his homeland and began the great adventure that held vital consequences not only for himself but for all mankind.

A Covenant

During Abram's travels, Yahweh repeated his promises to him on several different occasions in order to reassure him and to teach him something about this new Lord who had claimed him for his own. (Gen. 15:1-20; 17:1-22). Each time the substance of Yahweh's message was the same, although the description differs. Yahweh will be the God of Abram and his descendants, he will give to him a land of his own, he will bless him with many descendants and will protect him from his enemies. In return, Abram must accept Yahweh as his God and follow him. This he does, first, by leaving home as commanded, and then, in an anguished test of his loyalty, by offering his son Isaac as a human sacrifice to Yahweh (Gen. 22).

This relationship between Abram and Yahweh is called a 'covenant' (Gen. 17:7). The word was used to describe a solemn treaty between kings or nations which fixed their relations to each other and controlled national life and policy. Since this was familiar to Abram, Yahweh used the form of a covenant when he invited Abram to follow him. At this time, too, he gave Abram a new name: 'Abraham.' This was a way of showing Yahweh's lordship over Abram; he had the right to give him a name and, to the people of that time, this meant the right to rule him. It meant that Abraham was now 'his man'.

Abraham and the things that happened to him are way back in the past. However, they are important to us because they are part of our own religious history and, also, because from them we learn something about the way God deals with people.

Three Elements

There are several imporant things involved in Abraham's covenant with Yahweh.

1. In these encounters, *Yahweh reveals* a little about himself. We know a lot about God today but that is only because we come into the picture after most of his plan has been spread out before us. Back in Abraham's time men knew very little about God, so whatever he revealed about himself in his dealings with Abraham was very important. To Abraham, he reveals that he is Lord of the earth, that it is his to dispose of as he will. He teaches him that he is also the Lord of history; that what happens in the world—victory and defeat in war, the growth of nations and their destruction —all this lies under the power of Yahweh who judges all things. Abraham first learned these truths from Yahweh's promises, but like the historian, he learned from events, too. In the things that marked his life after the covenant with Yahweh, he came to know a good deal about Yahweh's strength, his faithfulness to the promises he made, and his goodness.

2. *Yahweh promises* something good. We have already seen what this was. In Abraham's case, he begins by promising him material benefits and general blessings. He promises to take him out of one situation in order to place him in a better one. This is the beginning of 'salvation' history—the history of how God comes into the life of man in order to bring him out of misery into happiness. There is no talk of salvation to Abraham but, as God's plan unfolds, we can see that it was present even then. First, however, men had to be taught that something other than the life they knew was possible. Then salvation would mean something to them.

3. *Yahweh demands* something. The promises to Abraham and the invitation required something on Abraham's part. To make them effective, Abraham had to leave his homeland behind and set out on a journey to an unknown destination. He had to give Yahweh his obedience and loyalty, even when he couldn't understand everything that was happening. He had to accept Yahweh as his Lord, i.e., as the one who had supreme authority and rule over

him. This Abraham did, even to the extent that he stood ready to sacrifice his son, Isaac, to Yahweh. This is the first example of faith that we have in the Old Testament. Faith means to throw in your lot with God on his terms, to give anything he asks and rest your hopes on his word that he will keep his promises. Thus, Abraham is, as St. Paul calls him, the father of believers. God still comes into men's lives and invites them to leave something behind and follow his lead on the strength of his promise. People still accept his invitation and are willing to undertake a journey to an unknown destination at his word.

- READING FROM GEN. 15:1-12.

One of the special ways in which Abraham expressed this commitment to Yahweh was by offering something tangible to him. He also built altars to him at various places in his travels and gave of his possessions. (Gen. 12:8; 13:18; 14:18-20). In this practical way he showed that Yahweh was his Lord and that he had obligations toward him. These actions served also as reminders of all that Yahweh had done for him and helped him remain faithful to their covenant.

Yahweh continued to reveal things about himself in the events of the Old and New Testaments. He expanded his promises and brought more and more people under them. He continued to demand the same kind of commitment from men, namely that they must accept him as their God and give him obedience and loyalty. Men continued to build altars to him and to recognize their obligations to him by offering tangible things on these altars. God continues to deal with people in pretty much the same way even today. Christianity is the last and the fully developed covenant that God has made with man, and when he made this one, he promised that there would be no more. All of the basic elements are still the same but now they include so much more. As we continue our study of the Old Testament we will see how they grew.

After Abraham, Yahweh repeated his invitation to his son, Isaac, and his grandson, Jacob.

- READINGS FROM GEN. 26:1-6; 28:10-15.

The reason why Yahweh repeated the covenant with Isaac and Jacob was to remind them that what he had done for Abraham was not simply for him personally. It was for his descendants, too, and ultimately for all nations. Three generations had this truth brought home to them so that in the upheavals that followed, the clan of Abraham knew that its powerful God, Yahweh, was with them.

Notice how in Yahweh's encounters with Isaac and Jacob, the same basic elements that marked his covenant with Abraham are still present. He reveals something of himself to them, he promises them gifts and blessings and he challenges them to remain faithful to him. On their part, Isaac and Jacob accept Yahweh as their Lord and follow his directions. They also build altars to him and offer him gifts there.

At this point, God's plan is now in progress, and it is time to expand it some more.

Questions for Discussion

What does Yahweh's meeting with Abraham tell us about God?

What did Yahweh expect from Abraham?

Why should Abraham have acted in the way that he did?

What does it mean to make a 'covenant'?

What was the point of Abraham's making a gift to Yahweh?

What is the difference between God's approach to Abraham and his approach to man today?

What difference would it have made if Abraham stayed home instead?

Basic Bibliography

Salvation History, Neal M. Flanagan, O.S.M. (Sheed & Ward)

The Plan of God, Vincent Rochford (Sheed & Ward Canterbury Books)

The History of Salvation, Leonard Johnston (Paulist Press Doctrinal Pamphlet Series)

THIRD WEEK

GOD FORMS A PEOPLE

We have seen that Yahweh's approach to Abraham set in motion the salvation of mankind. The next stage brings more people under his plan.

Abraham's descendants, who are now quite numerous, have migrated into Egypt. As we open the Book of Exodus, we discover that they have been enslaved by the Egyptians and are being used for forced labor. Yahweh, however, has not forgotten his promises to their ancestors, and he intervenes to rescue these children of Abraham and to make a new and far-reaching covenant with them. The man he works through is Moses, the greatest of Yahweh's prophets in the Old Testament.

• READING FROM EXOD. 3:1-10.

Notice how closely this meeting with Yahweh resembles the ones had by Abraham, Isaac and Jacob. Once again Yahweh reveals something about himself. He tells Moses his name: 'Yahweh' ('He who is'). A person's name in the bible describes what he is like: Yahweh *exists* with such intensity that existence is his name. He also makes the same kind of promises to Moses that he made to Abraham: he will make the Israelites a great nation and he will be their protector. In return, he expects them to trust him and looks for their obedient cooperation in the rescue operation. They must leave Egypt and embark upon a journey, the circumstances and fate of which are largely unknown.

The Egyptian king balks at Moses' request to lead the Israelites out of the country. He wants to keep them as a work force. So, Moses gives him some signs of Yahweh's power to convince him that he should agree to their departure. The king wavers but refuses.

Moses keeps up the pressure, firm in his belief that Yahweh will keep his promise and get them out of Egypt. The last sign that Yahweh gives is the most terrible.

20

- READING FROM EXOD. 12:29-36.

Thus, the Israelites escape from Egypt and begin their trek through the desert until they finally reach the land promised to Abraham. Their 'exodus'—or 'going out' from Egypt—is such an important event in their lives that forever afterward, they remember it each year in the Passover celebration. The name 'Passover' comes from the fact that Yahweh's punishing angel 'passed over' the Israelite homes and struck only the Egyptians. (Exod. 12:1-28.)

Having left Egypt, the Israelites pass through the Red Sea, escape the Egyptians who again try to stop them, and begin the long journey through the desert which will finally end in the land promised to their forefathers. The trip is not without its difficulties. There is a good deal of grumbling and dissension among the people because travel in the desert is difficult and dangerous. There are several attempts to turn back, and Moses has to keep after them to trust in Yahweh's promises. When their food runs out, they survive by eating the famous 'manna' that is mysteriously provided. Exactly what it was we don't know, but they accepted it as a providential gift from Yahweh that encouraged them to go on.

Finally, after many vicissitudes the Israelites arrive at Mount Sinai in the Arabian desert where the purpose of their exodus from Egypt and their journey to the promised land is revealed to them by Yahweh.

- READING FROM EXOD. 19:1-8.

Yahweh's message to the Israelites is substantially the same as the one spoken to Abraham. The difference is that this time he is addressing *a whole community* and offering *them* the gifts which he promised their ancestor. He promises them that he will make a covenant with them that will set them apart from all the other peoples of the earth so that they will be his own people. Like Abraham, he asks something of them, namely, that they will ". . . hearken to my voice and keep my covenant." Like Abraham, his descendants now make the decision to throw in their lot with Yahweh and enter into covenant with him. Through Moses, in solemn and awesome fashion, Yahweh reveals to them what the terms of that covenant will be.

- READING FROM EXOD. 20:1-20.

This is the origin of the ten commandments; they are the specific ways in which the people of God are to obey him and live out their covenant with him. They are a kind of summary of the more important obligations that will govern their daily life. There follow a great many more rules and regulations in the following chapters of the Old Testament. These spell out in great detail the way of life of the nation that has now become the people of God.

When Moses has made all these things clear to the people and they have seen the signs of Yahweh's presence, they solemnly agree to do what Yahweh asks of them.

- READING FROM EXOD. 24:3-8.

The ceremony which the book of Exodus thus describes gives us an idea how seriously the Israelites regarded the covenant. Back in ancient history when men made solemn agreements with one another, there was a certain amount of ritual that they went through. This emphasized in their minds the seriousness of the undertaking. We still have the same kind of thing when the president signs an important bill into law. There is a gathering in the White House, the reporters and photographers are present, he signs with several pens that are given to some of the people present as souvenirs of this important event. In primitive times, gifts were exchanged between the parties as a proof of good will, and when the covenant was especially important, there was some blood letting. Either the parties to the agreement mingled their own blood, or animals were slain and the blood of these splashed on the parties and the covenant document. This is the kind of thing that we see at Mount Sinai. The terms of the covenant are proclaimed, the people signify their agreement, and animals are slain as a gift from the people to Yahweh. The animals' blood is then sprinkled on the altar which represents Yahweh, and on the people who are the other party to the covenant. The covenant between Yahweh and Israel was sealed in blood to show that it was very important and binding on everybody concerned.

Nation with a Mission

The rest of the Old Testament deals with how the people of God lived their covenant with Him. In a very real way the exodus was the founding of the Israelite nation. It began with their escape from Egypt, carried them through the desert to Sinai and finally into the Promised Land. This is why the exodus is so important in Israel's history and why we find them constantly talking about these events throughout their history, their prayers and their law. The Israelites became a nation through this covenant they made with Yahweh. Now they had a reason for existence. Their national purpose was to live as Yahweh's own people. Before this time, they were really only a slave tribe who had escaped from a tyrant. Now they were more—they were a nation, and one unlike all the others on earth, because they had been chosen by Yahweh himself to be his own people. Through them, he would reach into the world and carry out his plan for all mankind.

As in the case of Abraham, Isaac, and Jacob, we see here a repetition of certain very definite actions by Yahweh. First he *reveals* himself to Moses and later, through Moses to the whole people. In this revelation, he shows something of what he is like. He tells Moses his name, a name which describes him as the basis of all existence. He shows his love and concern for man by inviting these men to be his special possession. He shows his goodness by leading them to become a people who are just and good. He shows his power by the signs in the heavens that surround his action. Next, he *promises* them something—namely, a privileged position among all the nations of the earth. Then he *demands* something of them, i.e., they must leave familiar surroundings and a settled, though enslaved way of life, and start out on a journey that will involve unknown dangers. They must obey him and remain faithful to the terms of the covenant that they have freely accepted. Finally, when all this is settled, the people offer sacrifices to Yahweh. The same pattern of events is to be found in each of Yahweh's dealings in the Old Testament.

During the period of time that these books of the Old Testament cover, roughly 700 years, Yahweh is setting up the first steps in his plan of salvation. It takes time to do this because men must learn to live by new standards. However, Yahweh is patient and he teaches generations of men by repeating in word and deed the same basic lessons. Over the years they get the idea. It becomes part of their background, their thinking, and their history. Even when they fail, they at least know that they are failing, and that their destiny is a noble one. They know that things are different now.

God's plan has taken root and is now in progress. His people have learned enough now to be ready for more. The next thing that they must learn is *why* these things that have happened to them are necessary, *how* it is that their God must save them. This takes us for the moment way back in history to the very beginning of things, as the Israelites learn the background against which Yahweh laid his plan.

Questions for Discussion

What was the great importance of the exodus to the Israelites?
How was the life of the Israelites changed after their covenant with Yahweh?
What was Yahweh demanding of the Israelites in the covenant?
Does God demand anything significantly different from a person today?
How does ceremony help in religion?
What purpose did the ten commandments serve?
How, today, does a believer show his fidelity to God?

Basic Bibliography

The Book of the Acts of God, Ernest Wright and Reginald Fuller (Doubleday Anchor Books)
The History of Salvation, Leonard Johnston (Paulist Press Doctrinal Pamphlet Series)

MAN BREAKS WITH GOD

God's plan for opening his life to all men took a great step forward when the Israelites accepted his covenant. These people knew that Yahweh had come into their lives to stay. They knew, too, that they were the central actors in a very important drama that Yahweh was directing. But there were a lot of things they didn't know, and it was Moses' job to teach them not only about God but about themselves, too.

The questions that had to be answered now were the 'why' questions. Why did Yahweh get himself involved with the Israelites? Why was it necessary that he take a hand in things himself? What were the reasons behind his plan? Why indeed was there a plan at all?

These questions are pretty basic. They ask about the beginnings of things and God's purpose in creation. Like all people, the Israelites had some notion about the origin of the world and man that had been handed down to them from their ancestors. Like other primitive people, their understanding of these matters was a mixture of memory, legend, and primitive science. Moses took the stuff of their traditions and told them what it really meant in the light of their present situation. Even though he didn't know much more than the rest of the people, he was enlightened by God in such a way that he could teach the Israelites the real meaning of their traditions.

When the bible came to be written the Israelites remembered this lesson and put it in the first 11 chapters of the Book of Genesis. These chapters are different from the rest of the bible because they talk about things that happened at the beginning of human history, long before recorded history begins. They really act as an introduction to the Old Testament, because they are telling why the Israelites came to be the people of God in the first place. They are difficult to understand because we are not familiar with the traditions of the ancient world. However, it is not too hard to grasp the message that these chapters provide. What it boils down to is that God created man and the world for one purpose, and man tried to turn it into something else.

This is how the bible presents it:

- READING FROM GEN. 2:4-9, 15-17.

In a simple descriptive way we are told that God made heaven and earth and everything in it. We are reminded that man received his life from God and was placed in the world to take care of it and develop it. And finally, we are warned that there were limits to man's possession of the world. He was not its absolute master. The final judgment about what man did was meant to stay with God. This is the sense of what we just read.

Then the Israelites had to be reminded about something else. Woman also was a creature of God. She was as much God's image as man was and should be treated as such. This was a necessary reminder because in much of the world at that time women were treated as second-class citizens, little better than man's property.

- READING FROM GEN. 2:18-24.

This lesson points up the equality before God of man and woman and the fact that the institution of marriage was given by God from the very beginning. The names, of course, are fictitious because there is no way of knowing what they actually were. 'Adam' is the Hebrew word for 'man', and 'Eve' is Hebrew for 'mother of all the living'.

One final point is brought home very strongly in these chapters. Everything in the world came from God, and this means that in the beginning everything was good.

- READING FROM GEN. 1:28-31.

Everything may have been good in the beginning but after several centuries of slavery the Israelites knew that this wasn't the situation anymore. There was a lot of evil in the world, and they had to be taught where it came from. The bible tells what happened:

- READING FROM GEN. 3:1-13.

The story of Adam and Eve and their sin is familiar to everybody. So familiar, in fact, that we are apt to get caught up in the details and be distracted from the main point that was being brought home to the Israelites. Some things should be made clear at the outset:

1. The details of the story are unimportant. No one, Moses included, knew what this first couple actually did.

2. The description in the story is symbolic. That means that Moses told the truth about the beginning through things that his people already knew.

3. The garden is the kind of picture of a perfect way to live that would appeal to people who live in a semi-desert country.

4. The tree of knowledge of good and evil is a picturesque way of saying that God kept for himself the right to tell what was good and what wasn't.

5. The eating of the fruit is a picturesque way of saying that Adam and Eve wouldn't accept this limitation on their life and tried to put themselves in the place of God so that they would be the final judges of right and wrong.

6. The serpent is a symbol for the devil—that great angel of God who, like Adam and Eve, turned against God and tried to make himself God. Of course, he couldn't; but he tries to win men away from God and make a kingdom of his own.

God's Creation

When these things are understood, the point of this lesson is clear. God created everything and time began. To 'create' means to produce something out of nothing. Out of all the things he created, God made man the most perfect and put him in charge of the world. But man was there as God's representative; the world still belonged to God and man was supposed to work it for him as well as enjoy it. The sign that God was still the overlord is the tree which stood there to remind Adam everytime he looked at it, that he was responsible to God. Sin consists of rebelling against God, of putting one's self ahead of God. This is exactly what Adam and Eve did when they ate of the tree. They refused to acknowledge God's right to set standards of good and evil and tried to take over this power for themselves. They failed, of course, for God cannot be displaced in the world, and as a consequence, evil and suffering and death came into the world and made it necessary for God to act to save men from themselves.

• READING FROM GEN. 3:16-24.

The results were immediate. Adam could not rebel against God and be friends with him at the same time. The ideal life of the garden was over. They were put out. They no longer walked in the close company of God in intimacy and love. Life was no longer peaceful and easy. Disorder came in and even man's own feelings and emotions fought against him. Life was now a struggle.

Salvation Promised

This is the teaching that Moses gave his people about the beginning. Chapters 4-11 of Genesis go on to tell how things went on from there. Murder and hatred came into the world and spread swiftly over the centuries. Men lived with little attention and concern for God or other men and the human race declined very rapidly into a barbarous state. But God did not abandon man. Even though man had turned against his Creator, God still saw there was good, and he would not destroy what he had made. Instead he resolved to save man as he had promised.

• READING FROM GEN. 3:15.

With this promise of God, Moses brings his lesson up-to-date for his audience. He connects his teaching about the early history of man with what is now happening to the Israelites. He reminds them that right from the beginning God had promised that he would not leave men to the hopeless task of trying to put back together what they had broken. God promised that one day the descendant of this woman Eve would crush the power of evil in the world. Looking back we know that this refers to Christ. This was the origin of salvation. This is why there is such a thing as a plan of God for man in spite of all the difficulties and failures we see in history. This is why the Israelites had a story at all. They were a necessary step in the plan that would lead up to the appearance of that descendant of Eve who would finally break the power of evil and reconcile man and God in the same warm friendship that Adam broke by sin.

It was important for the Israelites to understand that their God Yahweh was the same God who created the world. This put him in a class above all the other gods they had ever heard of and it gave him new importance and power in their eyes. Moses knew that his people had to be constantly reminded of these truths because, like Adam, they were always ready to go their own way and make gods of themselves. What Moses taught his people about their distant background fitted in well with what they were learning about

Yahweh during their exodus and journey through the desert. Right from the beginning, Moses showed them, God had *revealed* something about himself in his close friendship with Adam. He had revealed his power and intelligence in creating a complex and wonderful world. He showed his goodness and generosity in giving it to man. He showed his faithfulness and love of his creatures by giving them this to enjoy always.

Love Rejected

He *promised* something too. He promised Adam that all this would remain under man's control and that the human family would grow and prosper. He promised man would never die and that he would always enjoy the good things God had given him and the companionship of God himself.

He *demanded* something from man for all this. It was a little thing. All Adam had to do was to acknowledge that he was indebted to God for all these things. God was still God and man must never forget this. He had to accept God's dominion over him, and respecting God's command about the tree was the tangible way in which he would do this. Thus, he would give God that recognition which his dependence upon God demanded. This would be his worship. This, and the faithful carrying out of his stewardship over the things of the earth. Unfortunately, Adam failed. And so did many of those who came after him.

Questions for Discussion

Why is there a 'history of salvation'?

What was God's original plan for man?

What was wrong with the behavior of Adam and Eve?

Do you think that there was anything unfair about the way God dealt with them?

What else do you think God might have done?

Why should the conduct of Adam and Eve affect us?

Is there any connection between the things I do, good or bad, and what happens to other people?

Basic Bibliography

The Image of God in Creation, Sr. M. Charles Borromeo Muckenhirn (Prentice-Hall)

God's Story of Creation (Knights of Columbus Series No. 48)

MAN'S LIFE UNDER THE FORMER COVENANT

When Moses taught the Israelites what had prompted Yahweh to enter their lives the way he did, the things that were happening to them began to make sense. They could begin to see that their rescue from Egypt wasn't something Yahweh did just out of the blue. There was a reason for it, and somehow it was tied up with his dealings with their ancestors, Abraham, Isaac and Jacob. These dealings, in turn, were tied up with something that had happened way back at the dawn of the human race. And now, somehow, the whole Israelite people were caught up in this whole process. Not only was Israel connected with what had happened in the past, but looking at the covenant Yahweh had made with them, his people could see that the end was not yet. There was a future to be worked out and they were very much a part of it.

Naturally, at that time, none of these things were very clearly understood. But the Israelites did have some sense of being caught up in God's plans for men and sensed that they were at the center of whatever it was that Yahweh was doing. They had his word for this.

Now that Yahweh had made a covenant with a whole people, religion became a little more complicated than the simple person-to-person relationship we saw in the case of Abraham. Yahweh's people were now a social group, and this meant that there was a whole network of relationships among themselves that had to be worked out and related to the basic charter of the nation, that is, the covenant. The ten commandments formed the basic law of Israel, but they had to be filled out with a whole set of other laws so that the life of the people might be organized and administered in orderly fashion. Thus the basic books of the Old Testament (the Pentateuch) contain the property and criminal laws of the nation, rules of worship and sacrifice, regulations about health and marriage. All of these were tied in with the covenant and the commandments given by Yahweh, so that the people could see that their whole life was a living out of the covenant and that everything they did was of concern to Yahweh.

People, however, don't change overnight, and the Israelites were no exception. It wasn't long after the first enthusiastic acceptance of the covenant that they grew restless and dissatisfied. They even went so far as to make idols for themselves and to worship these instead of Yahweh. So, Yahweh began the long process of leading his people through trial and suffering that would gradually purify them and confirm their faith. He kept them in the desert for a whole generation, toughening and disciplining them until they forgot about the fleshpots of Egypt. We don't have to look very far to see how important this kind of purification still is for the Christian. It is still necessary for him to discipline himself in order to be faithful to God and keep the attraction of material things down to size.

Israel's Homeland

At length, the Israelites completed their wanderings and entered the land of Chanaan, the place where Abraham had been led by Yahweh centuries before. They were home and Yahweh had kept his promises. However, before they could settle down and build cities it was necessary to clear out the pagan tribes that had settled there during their long absence. For the next two hundred years, Israel was at war off and on with these people until finally all of the land of their fathers was re-conquered and they could settle down and build a permanent home. Once they got established they set up a kingdom and found a king for themselves, and for a while, stability and order reigned.

I am going to pass over the details of Israel's history because there isn't time to go into them. The best way to learn about all that happened is to read the bible account, and I refer you in particular to the Books of Kings.

Suffice it to say, that at this point in history, you will notice that all of Yahweh's promises to Abraham have been fulfilled. His descendants have become a great nation, at least one that has an identity of its own and the respect and fear of its neighbors. They have a sizeable land of their own. Yahweh is their God and gives them protection, prosperity and other signs of his blessing. This, in substance, was what he promised Abraham, and now he has kept his promise. However, there was a good deal more to these promises than Abraham and his descendants realized. Yahweh planned to make of his people a still greater society and give them a new kind of kingdom and be their father and friend in a way that they could not imagine. Lest they think that what they had already received was all there was to it. Yahweh now opened the door a little further and promised to David, the greatest of their kings, something greater.

- READING FROM 2 KG. 7:8-17.

Yahweh promises that David's descendants will reign forever in the kingdom that he will establish, and he, Yahweh, will be a father to them. David probably thought this meant the kind of kingdom they had at that time, but looking back, we know that it refers to the kingdom 'not of this world' that Jesus Christ established some 800 years later. The Gospels are careful to remind us that Jesus is the descendant of David.

The story of Israel is really the story of how Yahweh's people lived the covenant they had made with him. According to its terms, Yahweh would bless and protect them, and this he did as long as they kept the covenant. He established them in the land of their fathers, strengthened them in battle, and protected them against their enemies. But Israel was not faithful to the covenant. They constantly forgot Yahweh, forgot who it was that had done all of these things for them. They broke his commandments and brought in the false gods of their idolatrous neighbors and worshiped them. They intrigued in politics with their pagan neighbors and got involved in their wars and conquests. The rulers of Israel took advantage of their own people, and poverty and injustice and oppression were common. Worship of Yahweh became a mechanical thing, animals were offered in sacrifice without any genuine spirit of sacrifice. When these things happened Yahweh sent prophets to call the people to repentance, to remind them of the covenant, and to warn them of the disasters that would follow if they did not mend their ways and return to the covenant.

- READING FROM JER. 5:1-30.

Only rarely did they respond to this kind of preaching. More often they persecuted the prophets and even put them to death. As a result, Yahweh withdrew his protection and let them suffer the consequences. They were defeated in war, suffered famine and disease. When they repented and recognized their failures and asked his forgiveness, Yahweh always took them back, renewed his protection and blessing, and they prospered once again.

However, the history of the kingdom is one of decline. After Solomon, the royal family split into factions and there was constant fighting over succession to the throne. Things got so bad that the nation was split and became two kingdoms—Israel and Juda. Now Yahweh's people were not only at war with their neighbors but with each other. Things went from bad to worse and the voice of the prophets grew more ominous, but they received little attention. Finally, the Babylonians destroyed both kingdoms, slaughtered most of the people, and shipped the rest off into exile in Babylon.

Faithful Yahweh

However, even though Israel was unfaithful to the covenant, Yahweh was not. He kept his promises and did not abandon his people even in their abandonment of him. He sent his prophets to them in exile and promised that after a period of trial and purification he would restore them to their land and make of them a new and better nation.

• READING FROM JER. 31:31-34.

Jeremia here indicates that something new is coming. Yahweh will not only forgive his people but he will make a new covenant with them and give them a law they will find in their hearts. Again, looking back, we can see that this refers to the law of love that Jesus later gave to the people.

During these years of exile Yahweh turns the eyes of his people toward the future, to that time when his chosen one, his messias, will come and establish the kingdom forever.

• READING FROM IS. 11:1-12.

This is the picture that Isaia paints of the new kingdom and the messias-king who will rule it. Everything is perfect and peace and security is everywhere. But there will be a price to pay for this in pain and suffering, and it will be the task of the messias to pay this price.

• READING FROM IS. 52:13—53:12.

After about 70 years of exile Yahweh kept his promise and what was left of Israel was returned to the homeland. They were a chastened lot now, poorer but wiser for their experience, and the community they established in Jerusalem now was a more spiritual and humble one than the proud and arrogant kingdom that had been destroyed. The temple was rebuilt and the law of Moses was obeyed once again. The stage was now set and everything ready for the decisive action of Yahweh that would begin the kingdom of heaven. It had been a long hard period of preparation and the Israelites had learned their lesson painfully and imperfectly, but now there was, at least, a small group of men who were ready to receive the greatest of all God's gifts—his Son. He could now come with a fair chance of being heard and accepted by his own people.

In the long history of Israel there were a few basic things which Yahweh hammered home to his people. The most important is the fact that he is God, and that there are no other gods besides him.

- READING FROM DEUT. 6:4-15.

Yahweh taught them this not only through the words of Moses, but much more drastically through the events of Israel's history. We learn as much from experience in life as we do in school. The same was true of Israel. We have seen how they had a tendency to forget the things Moses taught them and that the lasting lessons came from what happened when they broke the covenant. Throughout the history of Israel Yahweh had many dealings with his people. In those events of war and peace, exile and rescue, Israel learned what their God was like. He *revealed* himself in what he did for them and they learned that he was the one true God from the disasters that befell them when they chased after other gods. They learned, too, that he was patient, loving and faithful to his promises.

So, like Abraham, the Israelites came to know their God in the things he did. In these events, Yahweh continued to *promise* something. He repeated the promises made to their forefathers. He carried out these promises literally, and then he promised them more—a whole new and more wonderful development in man's life with God.

Finally, he continued to *demand* their faith and obedience. They were to have no other gods and they were to observe faithfully the commandments he had given them and all of the terms of the covenant. Their life, their future, and everything else depended on this.

Somehow, in spite of the many failures of Israel, Yahweh got them through everything and after almost 2000 years he had a small community, tried and ready, for the next and most crucial phase in his plan. This phase was nothing less than the complete reconciliation of man to God.

Questions for Discussion

How did their religion affect the everyday life of the Israelites?
What does the history of Israel teach us about human nature?
What makes idol worship so wrong?
What kinds of idolatry are practised today?
Why is hope something religious?
Why was Jesus so long in coming?
In what ways does God teach his people today?

Basic Bibliography

Salvation History, Neal M. Flanagan, O.S.M. (Sheed & Ward)
God is Faithful, Mother Kathryn Sullivan, R.S.C.J. (Paulist Press Doctrinal Pamphlet Series)
The Hope of Israel, Frederick L. Moriarity, S.J. (Paulist Press Doctrinal Pamphlet Series)

THE LIFE OF JESUS

At the center of Christianity stands the person of Jesus, the Christ. The Catholic Church and the faith and hopes of Catholics exist because of him. If you were to take away Jesus, the Church would disappear and there would no longer be any reason for people to be Catholic. Everything we believe as Catholics depends upon him. That is how central Jesus is. He is described by his followers in the Gospels by certain important things he said and did. We will look first at what he did.

Jesus' Birth

• READING FROM LK. 2:1-20.

Jesus was born in humble circumstances in Bethlehem, Palestine, around the year 7 B.C. (the confusing thing about this date comes from the fact that our present calendar which dates years from the birth of Jesus took the wrong year as a starting point). The Roman emperor was taking a census of his subjects at the time and this is what brought Joseph and Mary to Bethlehem. The Gospels describe great signs and happenings in the heavens when Jesus was born. This was not quite as startling to the Jews of that time as it would be to us because they knew that God in the past had sometimes identified his special messengers in this way. They remembered the strange things that happened at the birth of John the Baptist and further back in their history, there was Isaac and Samuel and Samson. So, Mary and Joseph knew right from the beginning that her son was someone destined by God for great things. The shepherds also were aware from what they saw and heard that this was a child who would be favored by God in special ways.

Even more remarkable than his birth was his conception.

• READING FROM LK. 1:26-38.

Jesus' mother was a virgin. Again, this was not as baffling to the

Jews then as it is to us, because they had experienced the power of God often in their history and they knew that remarkable things often accompanied the conception as well as the birth of a messenger of God. Some remembered how Elizabeth had conceived John the Baptist after years of sterility and how their ancestral father Abraham, late in life, was blessed by the birth of a son. This was all part of Mary's religion. She knew that God could do anything and that her son would be great in the eyes of God. She probably recognized that he was to be the messias promised by God to establish the promised kingdom for his people. And so, in her deep faith and trust in God, she agreed to be the mother of Jesus, and God directly created the child within her. There was no human father and this raised questions for Joseph, which were finally answered only through prayer and the strength of God's assurances.

There is practically nothing known about the early life of Jesus until he began to preach publicly to the people. The reason for this is that the men who wrote the Gospels were mainly concerned with Jesus' public career. They were part of this portion of his life and what they saw and heard is what he told them to repeat to the world.

Baptism and Desert Sojourn

• READING FROM LK. 3:21-3.

John the Baptist preached the need for men to repent of their sins and to be baptized as a sign of their determination to be clean. This was only the beginning of what we know today as the sacrament of baptism. The ceremony was similar, but the effect on the person is entirely different. Jesus was baptized, not that he needed to repent of anything, but in order to set an example of repentance to the people.

• READING FROM LK. 4:1-15.

God's prophets had often gone out in the desert to prepare for their work by a period of prayer and fasting. So, before Jesus begins his life work he, too, prepares in this traditional way. The devil is curious about him and, suspecting that he is very important in God's plans, he tries to distract him from his task. Jesus sends him packing.

The Apostles and Jesus' Ministry

- READING FROM MT. 4:18-25.

The Gospels recount many of the things which Jesus said and did in some detail. What they were and how they struck the people we will look at later on. In this short outline of Jesus' life we will go on to the next significant events.

Sufferings and Death

We come now to the most important events in the life of Jesus: the Last Supper he held with his apostles, followed by his arrest, sufferings, death and burial and their tremendous aftermath: his return to life, the visits with his followers, and finally, his ascension into heaven. These occupy a good portion of the Gospels because they were recognized to be the real point to the life and work of Jesus. What their importance is we will see a little later after we have examined them some more. For the moment, listen to the account of the events.

- READING FROM MK. 14:12-25.

The Last Supper was not just a farewell dinner. These events took place at the Passover time, and in holding the supper, Jesus and his followers, like the good Jews that they were, were actually observing the Passover according to the Law of Moses. They sat down at table and recalled all that God had done for his people in the past. Then Jesus did something new for them. He gave them bread and wine and declared it to be his flesh and blood. He also promised something for the future: a day would come when they would banquet again in the kingdom of heaven.

The Passover observance called for a ritual meal to be held in each home. The rules were very specific. The head of the family was to recount to the others what God had done for his people in their liberation from Egypt. Then they passed the cup around for a sacred 'toast' in memory of these things. The food they were to eat was always the same in order to remind them of the meal their ancestors had eaten in haste when God's angel 'passed over' Egypt on the eve of their escape.

This is what Jesus and his apostles were doing at the Last Supper and he surprised them by giving it a new direction when he spoke of 'a new covenant' and the meal as his 'body and blood.' The supper was both old and new. It contained traditional elements that were familiar and some startling new ones.

Official Opposition to Jesus

• READING FROM MK. 14:26-15:41.

The decision of the priests and leaders of the people to get rid of Jesus was not something they thought up on the spur of the moment. Right from the beginning, he had been a thorn in their side, with his public criticism of their greed and hypocrisy. They did not take kindly either, to his broad and humane approach to the sabbath laws and other legalisms. They saw him as a real threat to their position and authority, and as his influence with the people grew, they knew their days of lording it over the people were numbered. So they decided to get rid of him. Naturally, they had to have reasons. Convinced that he was a troublemaker—someone who was making trouble, at least for them—they rationalized that for the good of the people he had to go. They suddenly became very much concerned with the public safety and order and imagined all sorts of terrible things happening if this man continued to operate. Having come to this decision, they enlisted the help of Judas, one of the apostles who shared their sentiments, and this is how Jesus came into their hands.

However, they wanted everything to be legal, so the farce of a trial was held and they finally convicted Jesus of blasphemy, after he quite truthfully identified himself with God.

Pilate was the Roman governor of Palestine, which at that time was an occupied country. The Jewish leaders had to go to him because the Romans reserved the power of life and death to themselves. Pilate obviously was not very interested in all the fuss and seems to have been convinced that Jesus was really innocent, but he was cowardly and when they threatened to report him to the emperor for lining up with a royal pretender, he gave up and let them have their way. His name is forever connected in the Christian creed with the death of Jesus—something he was too cowardly to prevent.

Jesus was crucified like a common criminal in the place of execution—'Golgotha or Calvary.' This looked like the end of everything. All the hopes which the apostles had built up around him disappeared and they abandoned him.

• READING FROM MK. 15:42-47.

Jesus definitely died on the cross. The soldier in charge of the execution checked this before he left the hill. The legs of the others

were broken to speed up their dying, but when he went to do this
to Jesus, he discovered that he was already dead. Instead, he
stabbed his spear into Jesus' side to make sure. Then some of the
disciples asked Pilate to release the body for burial. He did this
after checking to make sure Jesus had died, and they buried
him.

Resurrection and Ascension

• READING FROM MT. 28:1-10.

The women came around on Sunday morning because they
hadn't had time to prepare the body properly for burial after he
was taken down from the cross. The sabbath began at sunset on
Friday and Jesus died in mid-afternoon, so they had just time to
put his body in the tomb. The law of Moses forbade them to do
any work on the sabbath and, furthermore, a Jew was obliged to
go through all kinds of purifications after touching a dead body.
So, after the sabbath ended, the women came out to the grave to
do what they ordinarily would have done right after he died. To
their great joy they discovered that he had been restored to life as
he had promised, and he spoke with them and reassured them.

• READING FROM ACTS 1:1-11.

Thereafter, he visited with the apostles and disciples over a
period of 40 days, reviewing the things he had taught them and
letting them absorb the significance of what had happened. When
they got adjusted to the fact that he was truly real and that he had
broken out of death, their faith in him was restored and strengthened. Then he prepared to return to his Father. He took them out
on a hill and ordered them to carry on his mission of teaching and
baptizing, and then disappeared from their midst for the last
time.

Questions for Discussion

What is the place of Jesus in the Catholic faith?
Is the virgin birth of Jesus impossible to believe?
What did John the Baptist have to do with Jesus?
Why would anyone like Jesus make enemies?
What opposition should Christians expect today?

Would Jesus have been more successful if he hadn't been crucified?

How does Jesus' resurrection change a person's view of life?

Basic Bibliography

Jesus and His Times, Henri Daniel-Rops (Doubleday Image Books)

The Person of Christ, Wilfrid F. Dewan, C.S.P. (Paulist Press Doctrinal Pamphlet Series)

THE TEACHINGS OF JESUS

The people knew Jesus during his lifetime as a 'prophet'. To them, this meant that he was a spokesman for God, that through him God was telling them something important, and this is why they followed his words and wonders. To us today, the word 'prophet' means other things besides this, so we would be more apt to describe Jesus as a 'religious teacher' if we wanted to give his profession.

Teacher or prophet, what did his teaching consist of? Very briefly, what Jesus had to say can be summarized as follows:

Announcement of God's Kingdom

● READING FROM MK. 1:15.

Jesus began his teaching by telling the people that something tremendously important was happening right here and now: the arrival of the kingdom of God.

What this meant to his audience was everything. This is what the Jewish people had been expecting, living and praying for since they left Egypt 1300 years before. This is what God had promised them and what they had accepted as their national goal over the centuries. What V-J Day was to the American people, the day of final victory over the last enemy and the return of peace, is only a small indication of what the arrival of the kingdom meant to the Jews. It was the best possible news they could hear; that is why it is called the 'gospel', an old word for 'good news'.

Although the Jewish people had been absorbed in the coming of the kingdom for centuries, they were divided and unclear about what it was. This much they knew: it would mark the beginning of a new era under a new and great leader sent by God, and they would experience new evidence of God's love for them and would be drawn closer to him and receive new gifts and blessings. The difficulty lay in this last part. There were all sorts of guesses and

42

interpretations about what these new gifts from God would be. Human nature being what it is, people looked forward to the kind of things that appealed to them personally, and on this basis formed a picture of what the kingdom would be like. Some thought in political terms, others in economic; some in spiritual, others in terms of worship and the observance of the law. Some thought it was to be exclusively for the Jewish people, others thought it would be for all. But all expected a new way of life from God, and this is what Jesus announced to them: it's here, and if you want to be part of it change your ways and listen to my words.

A New Commandment

• READING FROM JN. 13:34-35.

The Jews had received commandments through Moses centuries before and had lived by them, badly at times, throughout their history. The commandments were the law of the nation as well as part of their faith. Now Jesus told them he had come to give them a new commandment: they must love one another. Not only had he come to establish a new relationship between God and man, but a new relationship among men, too. What it meant he would show them later on when he went so far as to give up his life for them.

• READING FROM MT. 5:1-12.

In many of his talks to the people, Jesus described what the kingdom would be like. It wouldn't be like the kingdoms men were used to where the rich and powerful were the favored ones. In the kingdom, the poor and the humble and the little people would come into their own. All the values that men are forced to accept by circumstances would be changed and true justice and equity would prevail. Everyone who has experienced injustice and looked to God to give a better life knows what Jesus was talking about.

A New Covenant

• READING FROM MT. 26:26-28.

The covenant of Sinai was the constitution of the Jewish people. This is what defined their existence and purpose as a nation. This was the framework in which they lived and according to which their laws were made, their wars fought, their family and social life ruled. Now, Jesus told them he was going to give them a new covenant. This meant that everything in their life, both as individuals and as a people, would be transformed and receive a new direction and meaning. They were somewhat in the position of one of the new African nations that receives a new constitution that sets it up as a sovereign nation after a previous history of colonial rule. It is a whole new era, and the announcement of this was momentous.

A New Presence

- READING FROM JN. 14:18-26.

Under the old covenant God was with his people in a very real way. His presence in their midst was symbolized by the Ark of the Covenant which was first carried about with the Israelites in their travels, and later housed in the temple at Jerusalem. It contained the tablets of the commandments, some of the manna, and Aaron's staff. These were the souvenirs of what happened to them in the desert. It was a reminder to them of God's presence among them. They believed that the top of the Ark was a kind of throne over which God's presence rested. Jesus, having promised a new commandment and a new covenant, promised a new kind of presence, too. This was to be a much more intimate and personal presence than God's presense in the Ark of the Covenant. God, Father, Son, and Holy Spirit, would actually be living within the believer and the believer living within God. Thus, God himself was to be the new Promised Land for his people. They would now live in *him* rather than just in some geographical territory given by him.

Everlasting Life

- READING FROM JN. 6:32-40.

What this would mean to those who listened was that they would be raised up from death and live forever in the kingdom of God. This was truly good news, because for a long time the Israelites were not clear about life after death. Only late in their history, after they saw their hopes of political and material immortality disappear in the destruction of Jerusalem and their exile to Babylon, did they begin to understand that their destiny reached beyond this world. Jesus specifically taught them that his kingdom would last forever and that although death will come to his followers, it is not final and they will be raised up to new life. This, too, was 'good news'.

A New Vision of God

We have seen how every time that God spoke to man in the Old Testament, he revealed something about himself. He disclosed his power and his love for his people. He continued disclosing more about himself in the teachings of Christ.

- READINGS FROM JN. 14:8-11; 14:16-17.

The great new truth Jesus reveals is that God is a multiple personality. He describes himself as the Son and refers to his 'Father in Heaven.' He also speaks of the Spirit whom he will share with his followers. At the same time he makes it clear that he is equal to the Father and that through the Spirit they will all three come and dwell within his disciples. Naturally, this was not very clear to his followers but they accepted it as they accepted other mysterious things about Jesus. They may not have understood, but they believed because of their great trust in Jesus.

In the person of Jesus, God not only invites the human race into his life but he shows us something of what his life is like. It is a life that is fully lived by three different persons. They share completely not only what they have but what they are. This is as far as love can go and that is why St. John says God *is* love.

These are the central points in the teaching of Jesus. They are the topics to which he returned again and again in the course of his preaching. Like a good teacher, he kept repeating a few basic things in different ways. Many of the parables and other illustrations Jesus used describe one of these principal truths. As you read the Gospels remember to look for these, and see how often Jesus refers to them. This is a good indication of how important he considered them.

Questions for Discussion

What has become of the kingdom of God since the time of Jesus?

What does it take to be 'a good Christian'?

How does the Christian look on the good things of this world?

Is man any closer to God since Christ than he was before?

How is Christianity a covenant between God and man?

Can this covenant be improved upon?

How is God trying to change man through the Christian covenant?

Basic Bibliography

The Power and the Wisdom, John L. McKenzie, S.J. (Bruce)

The Parables of Jesus, Raymond Brown, S.S. (Paulist Press Doctrinal Pamphlet Series)

JESUS CHRIST, LORD AND GOD

We have seen something of the life and character of Jesus. We have some idea of what he was like and what his life's work was. We have seen enough, I am sure, to be favorably impressed by him. But what is there about him that makes him personally so important to the Christian religion? What is special about Jesus Christ?

The Apostles' Preaching

The only answer to this kind of question must come from Christians themselves. Only they can testify why he is so important in their lives. Let's go back to the beginning of the Christian religion and listen to the first sermon ever given in the Church. In it, Peter announces to his audience the importance of Christ.

- READING FROM ACTS 2:22-24, 32-36.

What Peter is saying is that this man Jesus, whom many in his audience knew and listened to, is not only the messias ('Christ' —the Greek word for messias) promised throughout Israel's history, but is actually God himself (the 'Lord' God of Israel—Yahweh). This is the meaning of the words he uses. This great truth —Jesus is God—hit his followers with tremendous force when they faced him after his resurrection from the dead. It is this fact that gives him his importance to men ever since. And this is the central point of the Christian faith: that Jesus Christ is God become a man, to live with men and shepherd them home to God.

The Roots of Faith

However, Peter and the others didn't always know this. It's pretty clear from the way they acted when they followed Jesus that they were confused and uncertain at times about what kind of person he was. This is only natural, because the last thing in the world anybody expected was that God would come into the world personally and meet men on their own level. The Jews were expecting a messias, someone whom God would send to lead his

47

people to his kingdom. But they never expected that it would be God himself. No one could anticipate that God would lower himself to this task and take all the punishment and abuse that went with it. Men expect God to be above this kind of thing. Consequently, it is not surprising that even his friends did not realize who Jesus was until they met him in his risen life. Up until then, they were impressed and, at times, awed by him. They admired and loved him, but they were a long way from realizing who he was.

Let's try and put ourselves in the position of the apostles as they followed Jesus. Put yourself in the crowd that listened to him, and try and imagine how the things he said and did would strike *you*. I am going to pick out a few typical incidents from the Gospel, the kind of thing that must have impressed the apostles, yet baffled them.

• SELECT READINGS SUCH AS: MK. 1:21-31; LK. 18:35-43; MK. 7:31-7; JN. 11:1-45.

The first cures were startling. The people looked at Jesus with admiration and awe. They accepted him as a teacher and prophet. But I'm sure that after a while they began to get used to it. Even the apostles came to take his mysterious sources of power for granted.

However, there were other things he did that kept them off balance.

• SELECT READINGS SUCH AS: LK. 8:22-25; JN. 6:1-21; JN. 2:1-11.

This kind of thing showed the apostles that they were dealing with an extraordinary person, and it scared them at times. Some of the things he said certainly must have troubled them.

• SELECT READINGS SUCH AS: LK. 5:18-26; JN. 10:30; MT. 5:43-4; JN. 8:56-8; JN. 3:36.

Curing the sick may have become routine but the apostles learned something about Jesus from this. One of the signs of the kingdom that the prophets had talked about was that cures would be common. So they came to realize that Jesus was the messias, and they looked forward eagerly to the time when he would establish the promised kingdom. There were, however, some other things the prophets had taught that they overlooked. These had to do with the price that would have to be paid for the kingdom.

- READING FROM MT. 16:21-3.

Even with this warning from Jesus they couldn't face what looked like the defeat of all their hopes when he was arrested and executed. The confidence and expectations that he had built up in them vanished, and the apostles were frightened and confused.

The Impact of Faith

Then came the greatest of all the events that they experienced— the resurrection of Jesus. All their confidence and hope in him came surging back. Their faith in him was restored and this new sight of Jesus revealed to them something else. For the first time they saw that not only was he the messias but he was God.

- READING FROM JN. 20:24-9.

This new faith was the reason why Peter and the others could now face the world fearlessly and announce to the people what God had done through the person of Jesus. This was the reason why they were willing to change their lives for him and to die for him, as most of them did later on. They had met God in person and came to know and love him, and they would never be the same again.

What finally enables anyone to believe in Jesus—to realize that he is God and that therefore all of the things he taught and did are vitally important—what enables anyone to believe this is the same thing that enabled the apostles to believe: coming into contact with the risen Christ. He is still here among us, and still presenting himself to men, asking their faith and acceptance of him. Men must still prepare themselves for this challenge in the same way the apostles did, by listening to his teaching, by studying the things that he did and by putting themselves in his presence in thought and attention. If a man does this with an open mind and humble heart, he will find himself in the same situation as the apostles, and at the opportune moment he will, in his own life, meet the risen Christ. He, too, will be able to say like Thomas with all of the certainty of newly acquired faith: "My Lord and My God!"

The God of Abraham

When this dazzling truth about Jesus was first brought home to the apostles, they had a lot of adjusting to do. They had to fit this new revelation in with all of the other things that God had taught his people in the past. The biggest adjustment was to fit this truth in with the hard learned lesson of centuries: that there was but one God—Yahweh, the God of Abraham and Isaac and Jacob. All their lives they believed this; and now they knew that Jesus was God. These things had to be harmonized.

Looking back they began to remember a lot of things that Jesus had said to them that they did not understand at the time, but which now began to make sense. They remembered how he had spoken of *his* Father, how he . . . "and the Father were one," and how he . . . "who saw Jesus saw the Father also."

- READING FROM JN. 14:8-14.

Slowly they realized something new about God—that, in a mysterious way he was even richer and more personal than anyone had supposed. They now understood that he was more than one person.

They knew the Son. He was their friend and companion. They knew the Father of whom he spoke with familiarity and love. He was the Yahweh of their ancestral faith. And at Pentecost they came to know the Holy Spirit. This mysterious God-person, sent to them by the Father and the Son as Jesus had promised, came into them and made them alive with the life of God.

- READING FROM JN. 14:15-17, 25-6.

They now realized that somehow or other in the mysterious depths of God, these three persons were all the same God. While they could never really understand this, they could believe it, and the Church has so believed ever since.

The Trinity

We are now at the central truth of religion—the truth about God. We call this truth the Trinity. It describes as best that man can, what God is like. We know that God is different than we are, but we have no idea really how different he is. Only God can fully understand God. The Trinity describes one of the great differences. The truth is that God is three persons. Unlike man, in whom there is only one person to a customer, God is so vast and so alive that it takes three people to live his life. We know their names because Jesus told them to us: The Father, the Son, the Holy Spirit. He taught us that these three persons are each God. They live together in perfect love and harmony, acting with one mind and one heart. There aren't three Gods—only one. However, that one God is three persons. This explains how it is that God can never be isolated or lonely. This is really all we can say about him because that is about all we can understand, and the only reason we know even this much is because God has showed it to us in Jesus.

Until we 'see' God face to face in heaven we will have a lot of questions about him. This is something that is inevitable and goes with being human. Our experience is limited and it is very difficult for us to know much about things outside of human experience. However, this doesn't mean that we have to wait until the next world for contact with the Father, Son and Holy Spirit. We know that God is everywhere and that he is very close to each of us. We may have discovered him already through prayer. What the revelation of the Trinity means for us is that we know more about whom we are talking to. If the Trinity is an active part of our faith, our life with God is that much enriched.

The Christian Message

Ever since Peter preached that first sermon about Christ, the Church has proclaimed to the world that the man Jesus Christ who lived and died and rose again 2,000 years ago in Palestine was truly God come among us as a human being. Because he is God, the things he said and did and the demands he makes on man must be accepted by all who become aware of them. He is Lord and Creator before whom man can only bow down and obey.

To those who do not believe that God joined the human race, Jesus is a problem. He was a problem to the leaders of his people who executed him for blasphemy. He said that he was equal to God and they couldn't believe this was true. To nonbelievers, Jesus must always be a question mark. This isn't surprising. How can anyone understand him unless they see the most important thing about him—the fact that he is God. But he is understandable to those who believe that he is truly God, and to them God gives life in his name.

Questions for Discussion

What is your own reaction to the story of Lazarus?
What do these words mean: "I and the Father are one"?
Why should Jesus' resurrection bring about such a change in his apostles?
Why didn't they see that he was God before then?

Without seeing miracles can someone believe Jesus is God?

What does it take to make someone 'believe' in Jesus Christ?

Does Jesus' teaching about the Trinity help or complicate man's search for God?

Basic Bibliography

The Person of Christ, Wilfrid F. Dewan, C.S.P. (Paulist Press Doctrinal Pamphlet Series)

The Good News of Jesus, Jean-Claude Barreau (Paulist Press Deus Books)

NINTH WEEK

MAN AND GOD RECONCILED

Note: This presentation is a little different from the others. It is a summary, a review, and an explanation of what has gone before. Because its material is treated elsewhere, this lesson can be omitted, if desired, without damaging the continuity and basic content of the overall presentation. It is placed here as one way of stressing the key significance of Christ's redeeming action.

God's purpose in giving life to man was to share his own perfect life and happiness with him. This is what God wanted for all of us, but man thought that he could do better on his own. Adam turned down God's gift right in the beginning and from that day on there was a separation between God and man. Man started on his separate way—a way that, without God, could only lead to disaster and death.

While man changed his mind, God didn't. He still wanted to share what he had with men. So, he began the long process of repairing the break. It was long, not because God couldn't solve it quickly, but because he would not force men to come to him. They must come of their own free will and because they wanted to, —otherwise they could never be happy with him. Because of this God had to win man to himself and he did it by being generous with men, giving them help in their difficulties and promising them more. He also attracted them by letting them see the kind of person he is—powerful, loving and forgiving.

Obedience and Trust

In each instance when he approached man, God also asked something of him. He asked man to obey and trust him and to be faithful to him always. Some men did this pretty well—Abraham, Moses, the prophets. Others blew hot and cold, for instance, the Israelites in the desert on their way from Egypt to Palestine. At times they were obedient; at other times, rebellious. The over-all picture, however, was one of continual disobedience, selfishness and unfaithfulness to their covenant. The result was the destruction of Israel as a nation and the scattering of the people abroad.

For a while, it looked as though God had failed. It seemed that men never could respond to him the way he asked. In a way, this was true. Pride and selfishness had become a regular part of human nature and this was the trouble. Men really couldn't meet God's demands any more. They were too divided within themselves. It was a tragic situation and it was from this predicament that God determined to 'save' men. That is why we speak of 'salvation' in religion. That is why the story of God's dealings with man is a history of *salvation*. It is why Jesus is our 'Savior,' (the word Jesus in Hebrew means savior). The fact is that because man failed to respond to God's love for him with his own loving acceptance, we live in a world that is largely estranged from God. However, since Christ, the picture has changed.

Perfect Response in Christ

In Jesus Christ, God at last found a man who responded perfectly and completely to his demands.

• READING FROM PHIL. 2:5-11.

In his life, and particularly in his heroic death, Jesus acted completely out of love and obedience to his Father. This is what his Father wanted, this is why the Son had come into the world, this is what he would do:

• READING FROM JN. 4:34.

He would do this no matter what it cost him. No pride, or arrogance or selfishness was found in him. He lived only for God and by his life and death he acted the way man should have always acted: he put God first in all things, even when it cost him his life. The things that happened to Jesus, especially his death and suffering, were not the decisive things. These only happened because of the people who were around him—all the proud, selfish and cruel men to whom he was a contradiction. The thing that counted with God was his steadfastness and his humility and his unfailing obedience through it all. Because of this, God raised him up from death and set him up in glory forever.

What made it possible for Jesus, and Jesus alone, to make this heroic response to what his Father asked, was the fact that he was himself free of sin. His whole life was untouched by the selfishness and greed that was all around him. He lived a human life and was not corrupted by it. He brought the tremendous love and generosity of God into the life of man and in so doing, he changed the course of human life. What man could never do by himself because of his sins, God did for him by becoming a man and showing men how they should act as men. Like everything God does, he did it well and thoroughly even though it cost him a great deal. He did it so well that from that time on it has been possible for other men to be reinstated in the life of God by joining themselves to Christ. Adam led man away from God. Now Jesus leads us back to him.

A New Beginning

Sin and its aftermath, death and disunity have been beaten. Man has returned to God. Everlasting life, reconciliation with God, man, and the world are once again possible for all. God has made a new beginning. Like the first time at creation, he starts with one person—Jesus—and goes on from there.

• READING FROM ROM. 5:8-19.

Jesus has been set up as the head of a new human race. It is still the same people, but in Jesus they are offered a new life. To those who accept the offer and take their stand with Christ, it means living the life of God with him in intimacy and unity forever. What this means for man can be seen in the glorious risen life that Jesus now lives with his Father. This is the kind of life he communicates to all who come to him. This is the new life God brought to his people in Christ.

Why did God condescend to become a man? Why did he put himself in a position where the selfishness and cruelty of man could touch him? The answer to these questions must to some degree always be a mystery to us. Why God ever bothers with man at all can only be answered by the fact that he loves us, and this is a mystery. But it was this love that prompted him to approach Abraham and promise him his friendship. It led him to gather his people out of Egypt and promise them a kingdom. And finally, it led him to come among men as their equal and invite them to come to him and live the life of God.

In the person of Jesus Christ we have a new covenant, a new

relationship with God being offered to man. This is the closest and most perfect relationship that we can imagine. It is the offer to share God's life: to live as he does; in other words to have the most perfect life of all. This is a very personal gift, the gift of life, and it requires a very personal relationship to live it. This means that the covenant between God and man not only has to be perfect but it has to be very personal. In fact it is so personal, this new covenant, that it is a person. Jesus Christ himself is the new covenant. He is the new relationship between God and man. In his person he unites the life of God and man because he is both God and man. He is the real live, walking flesh and blood new covenant God has made with his people. We enter that covenant like Abraham and the Israelites by accepting what God is offering. Only this time he is not offering a land or protection or any other blessing like this. Here he is offering himself and a share in his life and we accept his offer by accepting Jesus Christ. This is our entry into the new covenant—our entry into Christ and the life of God. That is why Jesus is so insistent on the necessity of belief in him as a condition for entry into the kingdom of heaven. In the old covenant the test of Jewish fidelity was their obedience to its terms. God is offering man a new covenant and this covenant is Jesus Christ himself—the God-man. The test of fidelity to the Christian covenant is fidelity to Jesus Christ. If anyone would enter this covenant he must do so by accepting its terms—he must accept Jesus.

Revelation, Promise and Demand

Once again we see all of the familiar signs of God's plan. He *reveals* something of himself in Jesus. In fact, he reveals all of himself, for here he is showing himself in person, and we learn as much as man can about God. He reveals himself and he *promises* something—everlasting life with this person in the kingdom of heaven. Through Jesus, He *demands* something—faith and obedience to Christ—acceptance of *him* and putting him first in our life, for this is what the life of God is like: God comes first and if we would live it we must live it the way God does.

In Jesus, the plan of God takes a great leap forward. Man and God are as close together as they can ever become. Now it remains for God to extend this life of union with men beyond Jesus to others in order that his new and everlasting covenant can embrace all men.

When men discover this and accept it they enter the way of their salvation. They live by the Spirit of God in Christ and nothing but their own arrogance can take them out of it. This is what it means to be saved. Our sins are forgiven, we are reconciled to God, and we begin right now to live his life with him. We look forward to resurrection and glory and eternal life in heaven with God as his children.

Questions for Discussion

Why is 'salvation' so prominent in the Christian religion?

What is there about the human condition that keeps man away from God?

How did God bring about the salvation of men?

What did Jesus do that no one else did?

How did God react to the actions of Jesus?

What must a person do to be 'saved'?

What is the situation of the human race since Christ?

Basic Bibliography

Life in Christ, Barnabas Ahern, C.P. (Paulist Press Doctrinal Pamphlet Series)

The Redemption, Marcel van Caster, S.J. (Paulist Press Deus Books)

THE CHURCH OF CHRIST

God's plan to draw all men to himself has been in operation now for thousands of years. During that time some events have been key points in the plan. Things like the call of Abraham, the exodus of the Israelites from Egypt and their covenant with Yahweh, and most important, the life, death and resurrection of Jesus —all these were crucial to the plan. These events all occurred a long time ago. However, God's plan is not a thing of the past. It is very active in the present, too, and we are every bit as involved in it as were Abraham and Moses and the apostles. Today we are going to see another key step in God's plan as he unfolded it in history—the establishment of the Church. This is one of the critical steps in the plan because it is through the Church that the plan reaches us today.

Ever since God became man in Jesus Christ, the executor of the plan is Jesus. This is one of the reasons why God became man—so that he could work out in plain view of men and make it easier for them to understand what he is doing. From now on we no longer speak of 'Yahweh' but of Jesus Christ, because it is in him that God deals with his people. The first thing we have to say about God's actions in Christ is that Jesus formed a new people. This people is what we call the Church.

In order to understand something of what the Church really is, it is helpful to watch Jesus forming his people during his life on earth. Let's listen now to a few Gospel descriptions of how Jesus gathered together the elements he needed and formed them into what we now know as the Church.

The first thing he did was call his people together. Actually, he spoke to all of Israel, as God wanted to gather all his people around Jesus. However, not all accepted him and only a minority came to believe in him.

• READING FROM JN. 1:35-46.

This is the Gospel description of how Jesus gathered his first followers, the apostles. There were, however, many other people who gathered around him as he continued his teaching. We see them in the crowds that followed him. Most of these are unknown to us by name but they, too, made up that group of followers of Jesus who later became the Church.

It's not enough just to assemble people. There are thousands of such groups. What set this people apart from other groups was the intimate life with God Jesus opened to them.

- READING FROM JN. 17:20-26.

Every people has a particular spirit and way of life, and this is true of the Church as well. The Church's life is a personal sharing of life with God.

Jesus also gave his people a special task to perform.

- READINGS FROM MT. 5:13-16; 28:18-20.

The task of this new people of God is to make disciples of the whole world. In other words, they must go on doing exactly what Jesus was doing during his lifetime with them. They must teach men about God and what they must do to reach him; then, when men show their willingness to accept the gift of Jesus, it is given to them by baptism. We will look into the meaning and importance of baptism shortly.

The Church, then, is a group of believers in Jesus who are assembled for a common purpose. In order to carry out that purpose, Jesus gave them some explicit directions about the kind of things they must do if they are to make disciples of the world.

Teach and Baptize

First, they must teach the things he taught. Then they must baptize. Also, they must do what he did the night before he died when they sat with him at table.

- READING FROM 1 COR. 11:23-6.

We will see much more about this greatest of gifts from God to his people later on. It is enough now to notice that this is one of the activities which Jesus assigned to his Church to do in remembrance of him.

Another power he gave them to use was the power of forgiveness.

● READING FROM JN. 20:19-23.

Here was something else they must do in his name: forgive the sins of men. You will notice in these incidents the kind of thing that you know the Church does as a matter of practice.

There are some other familiar features which Jesus spoke of, too.

Every people has laws that order their life. The Church of Christ is no exception. However, Jesus kept it simple. He was setting up a Church for all men, and it was being established in order to bring them to God. This meant that it had to show the presence of God and his loving hand in its operations. So, he gave his Church only one law—the same law by which God lives—the law of love. It is a total law that enters into all of human relationships, and it is a demanding one. But it is the way God lives and invites men to live.

● READING FROM JN. 13:33-35.

Every people needs some government. This is true of the Church of Christ also. Jesus picked the apostles to exercise his authority in his absence and to take charge of his people.

● READING FROM MK. 3:13-19.

He also designated Peter to be the leader among the twelve.

● READING FROM MT. 16:13-19.

Then He showed them how they were to exercise their authority.

● READING FROM JN. 13:2-17.

A people whose law is love, if it is to be faithful to this law must serve others in truth and love.

The apostles were interested naturally enough in the future of this new people God had formed. Jesus left this open and refused to tell them when the kingdom would be completed. But he indicated it would be the last decisive event in the history of man and that when the end came they would know it by his return to judge them. Meanwhile, they must always be ready.

● READING FROM MK. 13:24-37.

We have seen how Jesus assembled the people that made up his

Church, how he gave authority to them and to Peter. We saw, too, how he gave them a task to do and a series of particular activities —teaching, baptizing, forgiving sins, celebrating the eucharist— that they must carry out. We saw how he gave them a law: they must love God and one another. These things taken together make up the structure and program of the Church. They must do all of these things faithfully and without fail until the time when he will return in glory to judge men and establish the kingdom in its final form forever.

What will keep this people together in unity and be the center of their life is the person of Jesus. His memory, his teachings, his example, and all the great things that he did—especially his death, resurrection and ascension—these are what shape the life, action and hopes of his people. To insure that this would always be so, Jesus promised that he would keep these things alive in their minds and hearts always.

- READING FROM JN. 14:23-26.

Israel had kept alive the great things that Yahweh had done for his people in the past. The prophets and men who wrote the Old Testament were inspired by Yahweh to remind his people of his dealings with them and his promises. Now, Jesus does the same for his Church. He promises that his Spirit will remind them of all that he did and taught. His people can thus be faithful to the charge he has given them and they will always be a light to the world to lead men to God.

In these Gospel incidents we can see all of the basic elements of the Israelite people of the Old Testament and also of the Church as we know it today. However, there still isn't anything startlingly original about all of this. There is still nothing to indicate that the Church is central to the plan of God for reaching all men. There doesn't seem to be any particular way in which the Church acts to bring man closer to God than he was before. What, then, is missing?

This brings us to the last and the most important ingredient that Christ gave his people. This ingredient is nothing less than God himself. What Jesus did during his lifetime, as we indicated, was to assemble all of the materials of the Church. What he was really doing was building a new and abiding home for God among his people. In the Old Testament, you will remember, Yahweh made a covenant with the Israelites by which they became his people. He formed them into a nation that lived by his promises and he was with them in some mysterious way. He promised his protection and guidance if they would be faithful to the terms of the covenant. He was present in his promises and this presence was symbolized by the Ark of the Covenant which accompanied his people in all of their travels.

Intimate Presence

Now, under the New Testament when God and man have come so much closer together, we might expect that there would be a new and more vital presence of God amongst his people. There is. The covenant is much more intimate, the law more demanding, the relationship between God and man more personal. With this, as we might expect, comes also a new and closer presence of God. He now lives not only *among* his people but dwells *within* each of them personally as well. This is the last ingredient of the Church and this is the last great event of the Christian exodus. The coming of the Holy Spirit or God moving into the people that is his Church and giving them his own life and action.

- READING FROM ACTS 2:1-21.

This is the beginning of the life of the Church. Now that God truly lived in the followers of Christ, they became the key to his plan. Through them, in something of the same way that he did through Jesus, He advances his plan by gathering more and more people under it. This is why he established his Church—so that through his people he could reach all men and invite them to follow him also. The Book of Acts shows us the community of Jesus' followers doing for the first time the things he commanded them. They teach and they baptize. As we follow the story of Acts in its account of the life of the early Church, we also find them doing all of the other things that Jesus had directed. And so it has been ever since right down to what I am doing today—teaching you what I myself have received through the Church.

None of us Catholics believe that it is possible to live our life with God without our Church. The Church is where we met God. It is where, like Abraham, we heard his invitation. It is where, like the apostles, we came to believe in Jesus Christ the Son of God, because we somehow saw him in the Church. Finally, it is where, as on Pentecost, God took up residence in each of us and in all of us together. Then we began to live the life of God. That's why we believe the Church is essential. It is our own entry into the history of salvation.

Questions for Discussion

What is the origin of the Church?

What is the connection between the Christian Church and Israel?

What does the unity of the Church come from?

What is the mission of the Church?

In what ways is the Church an advance over what God had previously done?

What is new and what is old about the Church's speaking for God?

What is the necessity of the Church?

Basic Bibliography

The Constitution on the Church, (Paulist Press Deus Books)

The Church in the New Testament, Thomas L. Sheridan, S.J. (Paulist Press Doctrinal Pamphlet Series)

BAPTISM INTO CHRIST

In our study of the Christian religion we have been occupied with certain actions and events in the history of mankind. We have looked at things God has done and things men have done. This is the way that God unfolded his plan before men. He didn't just preach at them, but he taught them through a series of important events that changed their lives. We saw how he came into the lives of Abraham, Moses and the Israelite people, the apostles and other followers of Jesus. He came into their lives and revealed a little bit about himself. He held out a promise of something wonderfully good and then challenged them to do something. Over the period of the bible—about 2000 years—God consistently acted in this way. The presence of the Church and its continuing activities is a sure sign that he is still present, active, and faithful to his promises.

From now on we will be studying the things that God is doing *now,* rather than concentrating on the things he has done in the past. However, they are closely related. The history of salvation is still being written. The things that God is doing today are of a piece with the things he has done before. Every time he enters a person's life today and puts the challenge to him and gets a response, another chapter in the history of salvation is begun and God's plan advances that much further toward completion.

God Enters Our Lives

We become personally involved in the history of salvation when God enters our own personal life in a way that we can recognize and respond to. When he does that his actions become part of our own personal history as well as important events in the history of mankind. The striking thing about this is how much of a resemblance there is between the way Christ approaches us and the way we see Yahweh approaching Abraham and the rest. Through his Church, Christ speaks to us in some way and shows something of himself to us. Then we learn of what he promises to give us and become aware that something is expected of us. At that point we are standing in the position of Abraham—facing the unknown with some fear and uncertainty, yet fired with hope and expectation of a better life with God beyond our present existence. We respond positively, by faith.

Faith is the full acceptance of Jesus Christ and his invitation to us. Like Abraham, we say 'yes' to God and hold ourselves in readiness to do what he tells us. And the first thing we must do, as we know from Jesus, is to be baptized. The word 'baptism' means to immerse in water. Christian baptism makes this washing an avenue to God.

* READING FROM JN. 3:1-8.

Jesus tells us that baptism is a rebirth—a rebirth in the Spirit. When we are born into this world we begin to live, and when we are baptized, we begin to live the life of God. Like the apostles at Pentecost, we become the dwelling place of God. He comes to us and takes up residence in us and draws us into his own life. We are truly re-born—this time as sons of God, sharing all that he has and is. Baptism is the first installment delivery of God's promised gifts.

Baptism is not so much something we do; rather, it is something Jesus does to us. Faith is the way a person gives himself over to Christ and becomes his disciple, and baptism is the action by which Christ takes a person into his life and makes him his own. For us, then, baptism is a key event in our own personal history of salvation. It is also an important event in the general history of man's salvation because it means that in the big picture things have moved ahead that much further.

God Liberates His People

Baptism is not only a rebirth and a new beginning. It is also a liberation. Yahweh not only led the Israelites into a land of their own and gave them a new start as his own people, but he also freed them from the slavery they knew in Egypt. He did this by leading them through the waters of the Red Sea to freedom. Christ does the same for us in baptism. He leads us into a new life with God, liberating us from sin and death. He leads us through water to do this. This is our own personal exodus.

Christ liberates a person from sin by joining him to himself in his own death and resurrection. These are the events by which he made his own personal journey to his Father. These same events are the way each of us is reconciled to God so completely that we live his life as if it was our own. Because of what Christ did and because we share in it through our union with him, God forgives all of our rebellion and selfishness. We are truly liberated from the stranglehold of sin.

Christ liberates us from death because he gives us his resurrection, too. We rise with him at baptism but don't experience it until later. Like Jesus, we must first go through death. When all have done so, then at the end of the world, all will rise from the dead as Christ did. Meanwhile we live his pilgrimage to the Father with him as we make his journey in our own lives.

Christ leads us into the freedom and life of God. He opened up this to all men in his own death, resurrection and glory. The human race gets a new start in Christ. When we enter his life what he did must be done in us, too. He makes us a part of these great achievements when he baptizes us. Acting through his Church, he reaches out to us and draws us to himself and into his own exodus, or passage from death to life.

- READING FROM ROM. 6:3-11.

We have said many times that Jesus Christ *is* the Catholic religion. St. Paul shows us just how much he is. I am a Catholic by baptism, and this means that my life is now so closely tied to the life, death, resurrection and glory of Jesus, that I live these things with him; I die with him and I am also raised up and will be glorified with him. He has given me a share in all that he did, and baptism is the first action in my life through which he does this. Is it any wonder that it is so important?

Joining the People of God

There are some other things that happen at baptism, too. Not only does Christ communicate his Spirit to me in such a way that I begin to live his life and am freed from my sins, but also I become part of God's people. God's last covenant with men was made in Jesus Christ. When a person is baptized into Christ he comes also under the covenant. This means that he joins the people whom God has formed by his covenant. He becomes part of the Church. To live in union with Christ in this world is to live in the Church, because that is where he is until his triumphal return at the end of time. None of us can live an isolated Christian life. There is no such thing, because Jesus is open to all and, when we come to him in faith, we find a lot of others who have done the same thing. God lives in them as well as in us, and his home is not a restricted neighborhood.

Jesus gives me some special powers, too, when he baptizes me. I need them in order to live the kind of life he does. He gives me the power to know, trust and love God and order my life in such a way that I will grow in all of these things. These powers come to me by the fact that the Holy Spirit, God himself, is present and active in me. He acts on my own limited human powers in such a way that I am capable of things I could never do on my own.

Jesus also makes me an active cooperator in his life and work. We will see more of this when we take up the subject of worship and the Mass. But just remember that a Catholic's part in worship begins with his baptism when Jesus takes him into a partnership of worship.

What Sacraments Do

In the life of the Church, baptism is one of those actions that we call "sacraments." The name is not important; it simply means a holy thing. There are a lot of holy things in the Church that serve as bridges to God. They are the contacts through which Christ communicates his life and Spirit to us. Seven of these are of special importance and are *the* sacraments of the Church. We will consider each of them in turn. Their importance lies in the fact that they are the regular ways in which Jesus comes into the lives of his people today and carries forward his plan for mankind. They are the current events in salvation history.

All of the sacraments have certain things in common. They are all actions of Christ. Acting through his Body the Church, he does something. All of them bring us his life and Spirit. They do this in different ways and for different purposes. All of them involve some public, physical action through which Jesus communicates his Spirit and life. In baptism, the action is one of pouring water and saying the words "I baptize you in the name of the Father and of the Son and of the Holy Spirit." These words and actions while quite ordinary, contain hidden actions of Christ that are very powerful. Like the cures of Jesus, they indicate something much more far-reaching and lasting than the action itself. They are the ways in which God is rebuilding the world—helping man to become the true image and likeness of his heavenly Father. It is truly a new creation because the sacraments bring new life to the Christian.

We call this life 'grace'. The word 'grace' simply means a free gift. And what a gift! God gives himself and his life to us as our own. Thereafter we draw on His goodness to grow up to Christian maturity. It is not our own doing but God's. He spreads his life through ours wherever he finds a door open. He does this through the sacraments and his other gifts. These others we call 'actual graces'—those promptings and consolations by which God helps us along. God enters into the life and actions of his people to make them truly a people of God.

Questions for Discussion

How does God save men today?

What is the connection between baptism and the events of the bible?

In what way is a person changed by baptism?

What persons are at work in baptism and what does each do?

What does it mean to be in the 'state of grace'?

Why is there more than one sacrament?

What happens to the Church in every sacrament?

Basic Bibliography

Baptism, Ignatius Hunt, O.S.B. (Paulist Press Doctrinal Pamphlet Series)

Sacraments of Initiation, Charles Davis (Sheed & Ward)

SHARING CHRIST'S WORK

Confirmation in Christ

God's plan takes into account the fact that there are a lot of people whom he must reach in many places and times. Yahweh started in a small way with one man—Abraham. But we saw how this beginning expanded into a whole people out of his descendants. The world might not have known that anything happened as a result of what Yahweh had done with Abraham, but the Israelite nation wasn't to be ignored. Wars, conquests and glory brought them to the world's attention, as did their defeats and disasters. And since all of Israel's life was hailed as the goodness or punishment of Yahweh, a lot of people in the Middle East came to know about Yahweh through his people. They came to know at least this much—that there was a powerful and effective God at work in their midst.

We see the same thing later on in the New Testament. Jesus too starts in a small way. There are only a few disciples in the beginning and the crowds he reached in his lifetime probably never were very large. However, once again, God formed a whole people from his followers, and the Church has grown enormously since. As in the days of Israel, the world cannot entirely ignore the Church. Men generally have been aware of this big group of believers around them ever since the early years of the Church. They have heard a lot about God and the salvation he brought to men in Jesus Christ even though most of the world still does not believe. Through his people, the Church, God reaches others, and this has always been a consistent feature of his plan.

It's also part of his plan for each member of his Church. In terms of all the people in the world, one person who comes to believe in Christ and is baptized is not much, but his conversion is not the whole story. God has plans for him and, when he is baptized, God intends to put him to work in the same work of salvation that Jesus is doing in the world. He does this through the sacrament of confirmation.

Witness to the World

The word 'confirmation' means a strengthening, and in the Christian life it means the action by which Christ makes a person a witness to what God has done.

- READING FROM JER. 1:4-10.

Like Jeremia, the confirmed Christian is not only entrusted with a mission but strengthened to perform it. It is in this way that the world has God brought to it. Confirmation makes us witnesses of Christ. Every Christian should be confirmed because every Christian is called by God to be a witness to what his Son has done.

- READING FROM ACTS 1:1-8.

Jesus' words were realized on Pentecost when the Holy Spirit came upon the apostles in such a way that they were strengthened or 'confirmed' in the mission that Jesus gave them to make disciples of the whole world. They began to give witness fearlessly, and many of their hearers were converted by the experience they had of the presence of God in these men.

The sacrament of confirmation does the same thing for each Christian today. It is his own Pentecost, at which the Holy Spirit strengthens him to be a witness of Christ and enables him to become the vehicle through which Christ reaches others. The confirmed person assumes responsibility in the Church and begins to live his Christian life, not just for himself, but for others, too. He doesn't have to be a preacher or teacher. But his life, his bearing, his speech and actions are now equipped to show forth the life of God that he is living in Christ. He becomes a witness to what he has received. By doing this he accepts the responsibility of being a Christian. He takes on his share of the task that Christ is carrying out through his Church. Since this task belongs to Christ, it is Christ who must give him a share in it, and that is what he does in the sacrament of confirmation. He sends his Spirit upon him for the special purpose of making him a witness, just as his Father did when he sent his Son to be a witness to him.

- READING FROM LK. 3:21-2.

Confirmation is given by the bishop who is the head of the Church in a locality. He gives it because, with confirmation comes a task in the community. The presence and action of the head of the community emphasizes this.

The physical side of the sacrament of confirmation consists of an anointing with holy oil and a prayer to the Holy Spirit. Through this simple action that men always associated with holiness, the Holy Spirit equips us to be witnesses to Christ.

Ministers of Christ

Finally, there is another sacrament that establishes a person's life in the Church. The sacrament of holy orders. A man is set apart for a special kind of life in the Church as priest or bishop, by this action of Christ. It doesn't mean that he is any better or holier than anyone else, but it does mean that henceforth he is specially identified with the holy work of Jesus. He is a member of the Body of Christ whom Christ will use in a special way to reach others. He lives to serve the people of God. Through him, Jesus will teach and communicate his life and his Spirit to his people. Through him, he will continue to lead his people in worship of his Father and to strengthen his flock.

- READING FROM 1 COR. 12:27-31.

There are different functions to be performed in the Church, so there are different officers to perform them. The so-called 'holy orders' are the offices of bishop, priest, and deacon. The bishops are the teachers and rulers in the Church. Together, they occupy today a place in the Church like the one filled by the apostles in the beginning. The sacrament of orders is the way that Christ equips them to be special instruments of his Word, his authority and his grace.

The bishops are teachers. As teachers, they are the official witnesses to what the Church believes, and they express the faith of the Church in what they teach.

- READING FROM JN. 14:15-17, 25-26.

The Holy Spirit enlightens the faith of the Church so that God's People always live in truth. In their teaching the bishops keep the truth before the eyes of the Church. They have the help of the Holy Spirit in this task so that their teaching always reflects the true faith of the Church. This is what we mean by 'infallibility'. It is God's action in the Church that keeps alive the teachings of Jesus. The New Testament is the teaching of the apostles, and sermons, catechisms, council statements, etc., are the teachings of today's bishops. All of these things put into words the faith of the Church. The bishops see to it that the words and the faith agree.

The bishops are also shepherds. They lead the flock of Christ in its journey through the world. All bishops share responsibility for the welfare of the whole Church. Most of them also have special responsibility for a diocese which is a part of the Church. In a diocese, the local bishop is the one in charge of this little flock. He is its teacher and its guide.

Bishops are also special instruments of grace. Through their sacramental actions, Christ communicates his life and Spirit to his people. They lead the people in worship and in everything that pertains to God.

Among the bishops, one of them, the pope, serves as their head and as the shepherd of the whole Church. Together with the other bishops, he has responsibility for all. He leads them in teaching and guiding the Church as a whole, and he, too, has the special help of the Holy Spirit to teach faithfully the teachings of Christ. As far as one man can, he is the chief steward who administers the household of God and acts as the visible representative of Christ.

Priests are the bishops' helpers. Under the bishops' direction, they lead people in worship, communicate the life of Christ through the sacraments and preach the Word of God. Deacons preach and baptize and administer some sacraments. As the Church has grown in size other titles and offices have been established, but they are only elaborations of these basic orders.

All of these orders exist to serve the Church. They are the social structures through which Christ teaches, strengthens and leads his people in the ordinary course of things. They are part of the Church, not over it and, like Christ, they are set apart to serve.

Questions for Discussion

What is the purpose of confirmation?
How does God reach others through his people?
What does it mean to be a witness of Christ?
What is the layman's responsibility in the Church?
How does God protect the faith of the Church?
Is there any real difference between a nun and a bishop when they teach religion?
Who has the responsibility to lead the Church?

Basic Bibliography

The Constitution on the Church (Paulist Press Deus Books)

The Decree on the Apostolate of the Laity (Paulist Press Deus Books)

The Decree on the Church's Missionary Activity (Paulist Press Deus Books)

Signs of Transformation in Christ, J.H. Miller (Prentice-Hall)

Confirmation: Gift of the Spirit, Mother Marian Bohen, O.S.U. (Paulist Press Doctrinal Pamphlet Series)

Holy Orders, Paul F. Palmer, S.J. (Paulist Press Doctrinal Pamphlet Series)

GOD NOURISHES HIS PEOPLE

History, we are told, repeats itself. This is true of salvation history, too. In the Old Testament we heard about certain things God did for his people. Now, if we look closely at the things God does in the age of Christ, we will notice how much alike they are to the things we saw him doing in the Old Testament. He follows the same general lines even though the actions are not exactly identical. It's like the artist who first sketches a rough outline of his picture in charcoal or pencil. When he comes to the actual painting, he goes back over these same lines, but now in a different way filling them in with color, and depth, and tone. The finished picture contains the original charcoal sketch. Only now, it is absorbed in a richer and deeper creation than could be imagined by anyone who had seen only the original sketch.

In his new covenant with men, God does the same kind of thing. Men already had the broad outlines of salvation drawn for them in the history of the Israelites. Now, God goes back over these lines and by his new gifts gives them greater depth and richness.

The main points of man's salvation were sketched in the events of the exodus. Just to quickly review them,—you remember how Yahweh picked Moses as his spokesman; how each family slaughtered a lamb and ate it in haste; how the whole tribe escaped from Egypt through the Red Sea; how they were kept alive by the manna in the desert and finally reached Sinai. There, you remember, Yahweh confronted them with the invitation to be his people. And there, they said 'yes' and made a covenant with him. You remember, too, how they sacrificed animals and sealed the covenant in blood; how they built an ark to carry the tablets and manna that would symbolize God's presence among his people. And finally, you remember how each year at the Passover they relived all of these things by acting them out and renewing the promises their ancestors had made to Yahweh at Sinai.

History Has New Meaning

This in brief summary is what Yahweh did to form his people, and from this developed everything important in the Jewish religion. It is the rough sketch of God's plan for man. Now, in the first century A.D., God goes back over all of these elements and fills them with new life and meaning.

Let us take a look at how God actually finishes out his plan of salvation.

First, he selects a new Moses.

• READING FROM MK. 1:9-11.

Jesus is, of course, the one he chose. He planned from the beginning that his Son would lead his people back to him. No one else could do it adequately, for it required the direct intervention of God to set things right in the world again.

There is also a Christian exodus. Remember that the Israelites' exodus included roughly everything that happened from the time they escaped from Egypt until they finally arrived in Palestine years later.

The new exodus covers Jesus' life journey through death to resurrection.

• READINGS FROM JN. 16:5-22; LK. 23:44-6; MT. 28:1-10; LK. 24:50-3.

His passage is not just out of Egyptian slavery and his destination is not just Palestine. His passage is from death to life; his destination is reunion with his heavenly Father and a human share in the life of God in heaven. Baptism brings each Christian into this passage and destination of Christ. Like the Old Testament exodus, Christ's too, was preceded by a special meal. And like the Old Testament, this meal is continually repeated afterwards to celebrate Christ's exodus.

• READING FROM LK. 22:14-18.

In fact, as the Gospel indicates, the occasion of this new Christian meal was actually the Passover, the day on which the Jews each year sit down to supper to celebrate the original exodus from Egypt. They celebrate it by eating the same supper their ancestors ate on that memorable evening.

God deliberately picks this very same occasion for the beginning of the Christian Passover. As the Israelites ate a special meal the night before their liberation from Egypt, Jesus and his followers eat another, even more special meal, in the same circumstances, the night before he makes his journey through death to eternal life. This journey too will free men; it will liberate them from sin and death. It is a similar occasion, and the preparations for it are also similar.

At the first exodus, Moses commanded the Israelites to slaughter a lamb and sprinkle its blood on their doors so their houses would be marked out for God's angel to 'pass over' on his errand of destruction. They were to eat the lamb, unleavened bread and herbs. Now, look at the food God provides in the finished picture.

• Reading from Lk. 22:19-20.

Jesus hands his disciples bread and wine but announces that it is really his body and blood. And he commands them to eat it. Thus, he gives himself as the lamb for the Christian passover. 'The Lamb of God,' as John the Baptist called him. His own blood saves his people from destruction.

Here we are at the heart of living Christian faith. This food looks like bread and wine, but we accept and believe that it is truely the body and blood of Jesus Christ. And we do this on the strength of his word. We eat and drink of it so that we may enter more deeply into his death and resurrection and have them become our own.

• Reading from Jn. 6:48-52.

Not everyone can believe this. But those who listen to God and are open to him can.

• Reading from Jn. 6:41-47.

This is the doctrine of the eucharist, the most important action in Catholic life. The word means to 'give thanks,' as Jesus did before he broke the bread and declared it to be his body. Somehow or other at each Mass, Jesus still takes ordinary bread and wine and changes them into his body and blood which he gives to his followers as their food and their principal and most intimate contact with him. How he does this we don't know. But the 'how' of it is unimportant. The fact of faith remains: what was bread and wine is now really and truly Christ's body and blood. (What happens at the moment of consecration in the Mass is technically called 'transubstantiation' by the Church.) And what matters is the fact that God feeds his people now, not with an ordinary lamb or the manna of the desert, but with the flesh and blood of him who is the lamb of God and the living bread that came down from heaven.

• READING FROM JN. 6:29-40.

You see now what I mean by salvation history repeating itself. In these events we see God going back over his work in the Old Testament and shading it in with a richer measure of his life and power. He picks a man, Jesus, to lead his people out of their deepest predicament—separation from their heavenly Father—and he asks him to make a perilous, apparently disastrous, journey through death to perfect, never-ending life. He also promises that anyone who believes in Jesus will make the journey with him. He marks Jesus' passage with signs and wonders as he marked the exodus of the Israelites. The journey is again preceded by a supper. The food at that supper is a 'lamb' whose blood will save the people from death. And after God has done these things he uses the events as the basis for a covenant with his people.

A Living Bond of Union

Remember that the covenant with the Israelites was the bond between God and his people, resting on his promise to protect them and their promise to obey him. The new covenant he makes with men is, as we have seen, much closer and more personal. It is not limited to words and promises now. In Jesus' passage through death to new life, God has saved man. And in Jesus' free acceptance of what happened, man has obeyed God. Jesus has made the words into facts. The new covenant is not one of mutual promises. A living bond of union has been achieved between God and man. Jesus is that bond; he is the new covenant. We become parties to this covenant by saying 'yes' to him. This is Christian faith.

Like the Jews, we renew our faith by acting out the events that saved us. The big difference is that when we eat the Christian passover, the food is the body and blood of the Lamb of God, Jesus Christ. Each time we eat his flesh and drink his blood we become more closely identified with him. This means that we adhere more closely to our new covenant, for that is what Jesus is—our bond with God.

And finally, the Israelites carried a reminder of God's presence around with them in the tent that held the ark. The tablets of the commandments, the manna, Aaron's staff—all these were symbols of what God had given them. But in the finished picture, God doesn't just give us symbols. Jesus Christ is himself personally present in our tents. (The word 'tabernacle' that describes the little locker on our altars where the sacrament of the eucharist is kept means the same as 'tent'.) We don't just have reminders of God's gifts. We have the greatest gift of all—Jesus Christ, himself actually present in our churches as the best possible reminder. We carry him with us, or more properly, he carries us with him, as he helps us along the same journey he made before us on our way to the Father. He is our food and the pledge that we will arrive with him at our destination.

This is why the eucharist is the most important act of the Church. It is the way in which the new people of God affirm their faith. They say 'yes' to Jesus, their Lord and Savior, by uniting themselves to him in the closest possible way—eating his flesh and blood and thus sharing in his risen life with God.

Questions for Discussion

Why does God follow the pattern of the Old Testament in the New?

How is Jesus' life, death, and resurrection an 'exodus'?

How do we become part of this exodus?

What is the new covenant between man and God?

How can we really eat the flesh and blood of Jesus?

Why do we do this?

In what ways is Christ present in his Church?

Basic Bibliography

Christians Around the Altar, Community of St. Severin (Fides)

The Eucharist, Neal M. Flanagan, O.S.M. (Paulist Press Doctrinal Pamphlet Series)

The Constitution on the Sacred Liturgy (Paulist Press)

GOD'S PEOPLE WORSHIP HIM

Worship makes us think of people praying, giving gifts to God, making sacrifices, and similar activities. However, these things are *acts* of worship. Worship itself is a spirit and an attitude that saturates the whole life of the people of God. They live in the knowledge of God's awesome power and unlimited goodness. Their awareness and acceptance of this we call 'worship'. Since this recognition of God's sovereignty is the foundation of all religion, then everything a religious people does must in some way be worship. The Church is built upon this awareness and acceptance, and that is why it is a worshiping people. In the language of worship, a 'priest' is one who offers sacrifices. All the people of God do this so St. Peter describes them as a 'priestly people'.

- READING FROM 1 PET. 2:9-10.

Other peoples, too, accept the lordship of God and in some way express this in their lives. We know that the Israelites continually offered animal sacrifices to God as a religious duty. Remember how at Mount Sinai they celebrated their covenant by slaughtering animals and offering them as gifts ('sacrifices') to God? And remember how they sprinkled the blood on themselves and on the altar to show how solemn their promise was? Well, God does the same thing in his new covenant with men, only he does it in a much more impressive and irrevocable way. We have a new sacrifice and a new sprinkling of blood. Old Testament worship is something else that God has now taken and enriched by the action of Jesus.

- READING FROM JN. 10:14-18.

The sacrifice that is now offered to God is Jesus himself. Not dumb animals, but a man's free gift of himself. What happened on the cross was that Jesus made an offering of himself to his Father. He accepted this terrible experience and turned it into a gift ('sacrifice') to God. This decision made Jesus' life and death one great act of worship. Thus, the blood that seals the Christian covenant is the blood of Christ.

- READING FROM 1 COR. 11:23-6.

What sets the new people of God apart from other worshipers is that they offer God the sacrifice of Jesus. His eventful life of self-giving was his worship, and our sharing in Jesus' life gives God's people also a share in his worship.

The life of Jesus is a perfect expression of worship. In him we see total dedication to God, a life of complete obedience and love that was poured out in willing service of his heavenly Father no matter what the cost. We know what such a life cost him. It meant his degrading suffering, crucifixion, and death. But it also brought his glorious resurrection. Because he gave to God total love and obedience, his Father raised man to glory. In this way, Jesus' worship became our salvation.

- READING FROM HEB. 5:7-10.

What happens at Mass is that his Church joins Jesus in his offering. We, too, become givers of his gift. At the same time we also make ourselves part of the gift by offering ourselves along with him.

The way in which we make this gift was laid out for us by Jesus himself at the Last Supper. He gave us his sacrifice permanently so that we could give God something worthwhile. Each time the Church celebrates the eucharist, Christ's gift of himself to his Father is there and we make it our gift too. In the Mass, the Christian community comes before its God and does what Jesus did before his Father. In our liturgy we not only remember certain facts that took place in history, namely, the life, death and resurrection of our Lord, but we also, through the power of God, enter into them and personally live them here in the present. We also enter into and share in the motives of Jesus that prompted his sacrifice. We thus enter fully into his perfect act of worship.

Stepping into the Future

But this is not the whole story. Not only do we live certain past events in the present, but at the same time, we take a step into the future. In our liturgy, we anticipate the final fulfillment in our own lives of the glory that the worship of Christ has opened to us. We anticipate even now our share in the worship which Christ at the right hand of his Father offers uninterruptedly in heaven.

• READING FROM HEB. 9:24-28.

How this can be is of course a mystery. It is the Christian mystery, and to be a Christian means to live this mystery with all of its consequences. The Church urges each Christian to participate personally in her liturgy so that each member of Christ will personally share in her worship of God.

The shared events are invisible, though present, but they are disclosed to us through certain signs. Thus, in our liturgy we employ things like bread and wine and oil and water as signs that tell us what is happening between God and his people. They tell us that the worshipful life of Christ is here in its entirety. They also tell us that we are now living it with him. They tell us, too, that we are part of the worship in heaven where no signs are needed— where all is out in the open.

At the end of days we will, face to face with Almighty God, perfectly respond with the total loving worship of Christ in heaven. However, at the present time because we are living and worshiping in this world, we share Christ's praise and thanksgiving in signs. We act our worship out in words, in gestures and in song.

While our acts of worship may be only through signs, our spirit of worship is not. It is exactly the same as Christ's. What we are expressing is not merely the meaning of what we are doing, but much more important, we are expressing our underlying obedience and service to our Father in heaven, joined to that of his only beloved Son, Jesus Christ. The spirit of Christian worship is the Spirit of Christ. His worship becomes our worship. His obedience, his love, his service, become ours. We worship God as Christians by putting on the mind and heart of Christ and reliving with him, through signs, the actions of his earthly life that expressed his mind and heart. Thus liturgy is for the Christian both prayer and action. It is a prayer in which the whole family of God shares—the prayer which expresses their identity, their service and their hope.

Necessity of Faith

It is impossible to worship without faith. It is by faith we respond to what God has done and accept his entrance into our lives under his conditions. Faith is our enduring relationship with God. It is permanent; it stays with us through all activities in the life and history of the people of God. In liturgy, we take this faith and put it to work in a particular way. We turn our faith to particular signs that tell us that Christ is here and now opening up his acts of worship to us so that his people can direct their sentiments of loving service and obedience to God with him. When liturgy ends one of the results certainly should be an increase of faith—a deeper bent within us in the direction of God.

The Mass celebrates the passage of Jesus through death to glory. It is the Christian Passover meal. Gathering around the altar table we remember Jesus' exodus. We also know that he then and there shares it with us. At the table, we do what he did the night before he died. In so doing, we experience both salvation and Christ's perfect worship of his Father.

Just as the Passover meal was the big incident in the life of the Israelites that brought their covenant with God alive to them, so for Catholics, the eucharist is the big event in our lives that makes our covenant, Jesus Christ, a living, present and influential fact. And just as the covenant made the Israelites a people and their adherence to it kept them a people, so Jesus Christ, our covenant, makes us a people—a Church. The celebration of that covenant helps keep us together. It also enables us to give to God the best love that ever came from man. And in turn, Jesus, as our food, gives us the love and strength to live our covenant. Is it any wonder Catholics call the eucharist the 'blessed sacrament'?

Questions for Discussion

What does Jesus show us about the essence of worship?
What kind of sacrifice does the Christian's covenant call for?
How do the people of God worship him?
What actually happens during Mass?
How are the Passover and the Mass alike and how are they different?
How does the Christian strengthen his covenant with God?
Is Mass really necessary for the worship of God?

Basic Bibliography

God's People at Mass, J. Richard Quinn (Benziger)
The Mass and the Laity, Frederick R. McManus (Paulist Press Doctrinal Pamphlet Series)
The Constitution on the Sacred Liturgy (Paulist Press)

Saying "Yes" to God

Salvation has entered the history of the world partly because some men have responded to what God has done. Of course, God is the one who saves. We could never become part of his life unless he reached out to us and drew us toward himself. But it is also a fact that he won't drag us. We have to do something, too. What we have to do is to say "yes" to God. We must say "yes" to his invitations.

We have a salvation history because people like Abraham and Isaac and Jacob and Moses and Peter and Paul said "yes" to God when he came into their lives and demanded something of them. And they went on saying "yes" even when it looked like nothing was going to come of it. They said it sometimes when it cost them a good deal. Some of them said it when it meant death for them.

Man says "yes" to God in many different ways. We call it faith when he says "yes" to the presence of God in his life. When we believe in God this is really what we do. We recognize and accept him as the most important person in our life. We call it love when man says "yes" to the tremendous goodness he experiences from God. And especially when he says "Yes, this person God is so much better than I that I can love him more than myself." And finally, we call it obedience when man says "yes" to God's commandments. "Yes, I will do these things that God tells me to do, because he is God."

These are the main ways—faith, love, obedience—in which man gives a real response to God. They are the ways in which man made it possible for God's salvation to find a resting place in the history of mankind, and they are the ways in which you and I make it possible for God's salvation today to come into our own lives and become part of our own personal history. We can say "yes" in big ways, such as turning from non-belief to belief; or we can do it in small ways, such as the small kindnesses we show to other people because God has commanded us to love them. Or, we

83

can say "no." This is sin: saying "no" to God when we know that he wants us to say "yes."

The Subject of Morality

This brings us to the subject of morality. Everybody knows that religion has something to do with morality. A lot of people think that this is all that religion has to do with. But you certainly know now that morality is only one aspect of religion. After all, it has taken us a dozen weeks to get to it. It's not all there is to religion, but it is important.

Morality has to do with human behavior. It is concerned with the things people do and the reasons why. It concentrates on the things people do deliberately and freely, although everything people do is important because of what it does to them. There are different ideas about morality, as you know, but the only one we are concerned with here is Christian morality. We are concerned with what Jesus Christ has told us that God expects of us. This is important because unless we respond to what God has done, it will never affect us personally. Jesus is asking something of me just as much as he did of Peter and Paul and James and John and his Mother and all the rest. He wants me to say "yes" just as much as he wanted these people to say "yes." So, it is important for me to know just what kind of response he expects. Let's look at what Jesus has indicated he does expect.

First of all, he wants my response in faith.

• READING FROM JN. 6:35-40.

My first "yes" has to be to the presence and the importance of Jesus in my life. If I don't do this, I won't get any further.

Then he wants my love.

• READING FROM LK. 10:25-28.

He also wants me to love my fellow men.

• READING FROM LK. 10:29-37.

And he wants my obedience. But with God obedience gets down to the same thing as love.

• READING FROM JN. 15:9-17.

God loves us, and if we are to be his children, we have to love the way he does. In the Old Testament Yahweh gave his people ten commandments. Jesus gives us only two: love God and love neighbor. They may be less in number, but they cover a whole lot more territory. We are commanded to love the way Jesus did, and that cost him his life. We have to love everyone, even our enemies. If we keep these two commandments we will be keeping everything that God ever asked of anyone, and we will also be making the best response that a human being can.

It is the best response because to love someone is to give something of yourself to that person. God loves us so much that he gives all of himself and his life to us forever. We don't usually do as well. We usually give little bits of ourselves to others and keep a lot back. But God wants all.

● READING FROM MK. 8:34-8.

He promises us that if we give all we find all. The reason is because God made every one of us to share his life. This means that if we are to be happy and to fulfill our potential, we must do it in God; and this means that we have to give ourselves completely to him. There is no other way to enter his life. God is a loving God and his life is one of love. Only when we give ourselves to him will our lives be full and will we be perfectly happy. This is how important love is in Christianity. It is really everything. That is why there is really only one thing we have to do to be successful Christians: love.

● READING FROM 1 JN. 4:7—5:5.

What makes it possible for us to do this in spite of the selfishness that sin has spread in the world is the grace and Spirit of Christ.

● READING FROM JN. 15:10.

United to Christ and sharing his life, his own capacity for love and self-sacrifice is placed at our disposal so that now it is possible to overcome our own tendency to self-love. As the love of Christ works in us we grow more like him and begin to produce good fruit as he always did.

Sin Is Selfishness

The failure to love is sin. Staying locked up in self and concentrating on self is the opposite of love. This hurts us because as long as we don't get outside of ourselves, we won't find our real selves.

We need to love to become fully human. And certainly we need to love God to become fully Christian. That's why certain things are sins. Certain things tend to keep us wrapped up in self and keep us from fulfilling ourselves. That's why God commands us to keep away from them. He knows that they will damage us and he wants us to grow into the life he is waiting to give us. So, even our obedience to his commandments can help us love if we understand what is behind God's command. He wants us to say "yes" not only to him but to our own happiness.

However, there are occasional failures. Men do sin. But God is still as patient as he was with the Israelites. We saw how often they said "no" to God. Yet we also saw how often He forgave them and took them back. He still does this. Every Christian become a child of God by his baptism. Even if he sins seriously and runs away from God, it is still possible for him to come back, if he will only turn toward God again and ask his forgiveness.

- Reading from Lk. 15:11-24.

Today in his Church, God still forgives his children and reconciles them to himself and their brothers. The action through which he does this is the sacrament of penance, or 'confession.' In it we see a prodigal son do the same basic things that the boy in the parable did. He returns to his heavenly Father and is made welcome. He repents. He changes his course and heads back to God after he has taken a detour away from him. He approaches him and confesses that he has done wrong. Then his Father forgives him and there is a big family reunion.

In confession, a person comes home. He repents and turns back to God even before he gets to confession. Coming to the sacrament is his trip home. He tells his Father what he has done and how sorry he is. Then his Father forgives him through the priest and he is rejoined to the family of God, the Church, and once again there is rejoicing.

The Old Testament shows us Yahweh forgiving his people countless times for all of their disobedience and unfaithfulness. Moses begged him to, as did other prophets and kings. But first the people must change their ways. They must repent. It is still the same. Jesus is always begging his Father to forgive us. His Father always hears this prayer, too, because Jesus gave his life in being faithful to his Father. But sinners must repent and change their ways. Then Jesus, acting through the Church, reconciles them to the Father. The priest is only the channel of communication between God and man. It is really Jesus who forgives and heals.

- READING FROM JN. 20:19-23.

And no matter what a person does or how often he says "no" to God, God always stands ready to forgive and to take him back.

- READING FROM LK. 17:3-4.

Sin is the human action that separates man from God. It is always a free act of man. There are no accidental sins. To take yourself away from God is always the result of putting self and your own wishes ahead of God. The only way to come back to God is to put him back in first place. This is repentance. It is the human action that makes it possible for God to forgive us. Forgiveness and the sacrament of penance are the actions that restore man to God. It is the great act of healing that Christ constantly performs for his people. His people are weak and always capable of sin. He strengthens them by the presence of His Spirit within them and guides them by his commandments and all the things he has to tell them through his Church. But men still sin. And each day Jesus performs miracles of healing as he reaches out and draws the repentant sinner back into the life of God and unites himself to him once more.

It is this kind of love from God that changes men and what God wants is to change them so much that they come to love him and everyone else.

Questions for Discussion

What is the connection between morality and religion?

What is the difference between a 'good' pagan and a 'good' Christian?

What does God want from man?

Which is more demanding: the Law of Moses or the Law of Christ?

How is sin destructive to the sinner?

Can there be any 'exceptions' to the Law of God?

Compare the story of the prodigal son and the Christian who comes to confession.

Basic Bibliography

Morality and the Love of God, Charles E. Curran (Paulist Press Doctrinal Pamphlet Series)

Penance, Thomas M. Finn, C.S.P. (Paulist Press Doctrinal Pamphlet Series)

CHRISTIAN MARRIAGE

The Christian life is living in union with Jesus Christ. He lives within each baptized Christian and he lives within all baptized Christians together. This life together is the Church, and man's life with Christ is the life of the Church. What Christ has done is to bring a new way of life into the world. Henceforth man can live his everyday life not alone, but sharing it with God—making God the partner of his joys and sorrows, his companion in the adventure and growth that is life. He can do this because in Jesus Christ God has deliberately entered the life of man to stay. Through his presence in the Church, Christ makes it possible to transform everything in human life into a loving gift to God.

We are used to thinking about our life with God only in terms of "religious" acts, things like prayer and worship and heroic sacrifices. Actually everything we do as Christians we do in the presence and company of God, and if we think about it, we can make it a part of our life with him. He had already done this on his part. He has picked out a couple of very important things in human life and taken them over as important activities in his life with us. One of these is marriage.

Marriage Shows the Love of God

Marriage is a natural for God's purposes because it is made up of the same kind of things that God wants in man's relationship with him. It is first of all based on love, and we know that if there is one thing that characterizes God's attitude toward us, it is love. We know that he loved us so much that he was willing to become one of us, suffer and die for us. We know, too, that there is nothing God would rather have from us than our own love for him. This love and the desire for it from the other person is also found in marriage. Furthermore, marriage is a union of persons; two people give themselves over to each other for keeps in a way that is more than friendship or loyalty or simple partnership. This is the closest unity we know of between people. That's another reason why God is so interested in marriage. He wants an ever closer union personally with each one of us. Marriage is a great help in bringing this about.

Marriage also has two people sharing a life in common. God's invitation to man is similar. He invites us to share his life with him in an even closer way than two human beings can.

Another important feature of marriage is the fact that it is through marriage that people are brought into the world and eventually into the life of God. So, marriage is important to God's plan for sharing his life with men. He looks to married people to help him in the progress and growth of his plan by bringing more and more human beings under it.

So, in all of these ways human marriage has a great part in the plan of man's salvation. It is the great example of total love between people and its presence in the world is a very real reminder that there is a perfect and enduring love possible. If two human beings can do this, certainly this means that God can do at least as well,—that the kind of happiness that perfect love can bring is possible to all people because God loves all of us.

Marriage has been involved with the history of our salvation right from the beginning. God created human beings in such a way that they would find happiness in each other. Thus they would learn the basic human truth that man is not meant to live in isolation from others but is meant to find himself in another person —in human beings in incomplete ways, and in God in a perfect way.

• READING FROM GEN. 2:18, 21-25.

Right from the beginning, then, God taught men through marriage that they were meant for others. Then when Jesus came, he gave marriage a new depth because the relationship between God and man got new depth in him. We have seen that the union between God and man that Christ has brought to us is the closest personal union possible. That the Christian can actually live the life of God with him as if it were his very own. Because of this the close personal union that is marriage has new depths too.

First, it is a sign of the union between God and man.

• READING FROM EPH. 5:21-33.

The love of human beings for one another in the Christian life is like the love of Christ for his people, the Church. This means that marriage now has new possibilities. It can bring people not only closer to one another but also closer to God. Because of the fact that two Christians are united each to Christ, this means that when they get married they each bring Christ and his life into their marriage too. It means that they share their marriage with him as they do with one another, and it means that they grow in love of God as well as love for one another if they work hard at their marriage. Christian marriage is not only a great school for the love of God, but it is also a special way in which God communicates his love and himself to the married couple. Each time that a Christian couple expresses their love for one another in any genuine way, whether through the marriage act or the simplest task of self-sacrifice and consideration for the other, Christ uses that human expression of love as a way to communicate his own love to the couple. This is the "sacrament" of marriage. Married love is a way in which God gives more of his life to us.

The Sacrament Continues

The sacrament of marriage goes on all through married life. It is not just the ceremony. The couple are the ministers of this sacrament all of their lives by the way in which they live it. Each party becomes the means through whom Christ gives himself to the other person. It is possible then, for people to grow day by day in the love of God through their married life.

Marriage is permanent because God's love for his people is permanent. He never takes it back no matter what man does. The married Christian reflects this fidelity in the permanence of his partnership.

• READING FROM MK. 10:2-12.

There is no divorce for Christians because there is no divorce between Christ and his Church. Both are for keeps.

The Meaning of Sex

Sex is an important part of marriage because love is creative. It was the love of God that created man in the first place. God was so good that he wanted to share himself with others, and since originally there were no others but God, he created people for this purpose. His love for us led him to give us new life with him even after man had rebelled and left God. Now, he shares his creative love with human beings so that humans at their best—when they give themselves to each other in the unselfish love of marriage—they too can be creative. The creation of other people is tied to human love, and this is one of the most important aspects of marriage. Not only does marriage bring out the best that humans are capable of, their most unselfish love, but it also gives them the opportunity to share in the creative work of God. That is why sex is so sacred. It is a physical giving of one person completely to another. It should express a complete spiritual gift of a person to his spouse. It is not something to be used selfishly for personal pleasure alone. It is meant to be used creatively and is a reminder that in the creative work of God, man's greatest happiness is to be found.

God expects people to live their life with him in marriage the way he does with his Church, lovingly, selflessly and creatively. He does not expect people to take on more than they can care for in a family, but he does not expect them to separate sex from his purposes either. That is the sin of birth control—the selfish use of sex and the exclusion of God's creative act. Man cannot share the life of God if he works at cross purposes with God.

His life with God is lived in the Church and he looks to the Church for guidance in his married life as in everything else that he shares with God. At the present time, there is much discussion about the morality of birth control in different situations and through different ways. There is much confusion, too, but the Christian looks to the Church with confidence that God will guide his people as he always has. The Christian can follow the Church's teaching in the certainty that God's life will continue to be communicated to his people in their married life.

God Challenges

Because marriage is the closest possible union between human beings it demands a great deal of married people. It calls for great sacrifices and patience and understanding and unselfishness. But at the same time, if a person gives of himself he will find great happiness and love. Happiness for human beings comes from giving. This is the great lesson God wants us to learn because our greatest happiness can come only from giving ourselves to the greatest of all persons, God. That is why he is so concerned about marriage. That is why he uses it as one of the principal means to bring men closer to himself. He uses the love of marriage, the sharing of life that goes on in it, the joys and companionship, the unity, the creativity—all of these things he uses to teach us and to help us grow accustomed to them so that we can be ready for our life with God. In that life all of these elements are present in an undreamed of degree, and man's happiness is total and everlasting.

Questions for Discussion

What part does marriage play in God's plan for man?
What is special about Christian marriage?
What important truths does God teach us through marriage?
Why can't sex be separated from marriage?
Why must marriage be permanent?
How does Christ communicate his life in a special way to married people?
What is the effect of daily married life on Christian living?

Basic Bibliography

Union in Marital Love, Marc Oraison (Macmillan)
Christian Marriage, J. Richard Quinn (Paulist Press Doctrinal Pamphlet Series)

God's Plan Fulfilled

Tonight we complete our presentation of the history of man's salvation. During the past weeks we have traced the main events that carried God's message and life into the life of men. We have seen how God began his plan, and we have emphasized the big moments in its history. We have seen how these big moments, and especially the life, death, and resurrection of Christ, have decided the relationship between God and man ever since. We have seen, too, how God continues to work the salvation of men through his Church and its life-giving actions that are the sacraments. Tonight we shall look at the completion of that history. Not the end, because salvation is never-ending, but rather the final events in the story. When these are over, there will be nothing left to be done. The relation between man and God will be perfectly stabilized forever.

There is one last act in the drama of salvation still to take place. Jesus has worked out the salvation of mankind, yet much of what he has done is hidden from all but his faithful followers. However, one day everything that has been accomplished will be revealed for everyone to see. Then all of the things that Christ has received will be fully experienced by his people forever. Man and God have already been reconciled in Christ, and those who accept Christ and commit themselves to him have already received the life of God. However, they live this life with God in this world. This means that they don't see God, that they live it partly in darkness, partly amidst pain and suffering and death, partly in joy, hope and happiness. But at the completion of things these limitations will disappear and God's people will see him face to face. There will be no more pain, suffering or death.

• READING FROM REV. 21:1-4.

At that time, Jesus will return in his kingly glory for all the world to see. Then he will not be the humble carpenter from

94

Nazareth whom so many failed to recognize. Instead, he will appear obviously as the Son of God, and King of the universe. At that time, too, all those who have lived since the world began will rise from the dead and undergo his final judgment.

- READING FROM 1 THESS. 4:13-18.

Death, you remember, is a result of sin. But once Jesus overcame sin, the days of death were numbered. Christ broke through death in his resurrection, and on the last day he will communicate personal resurrection to all his people, too. Men will be reunited in their own selves, as their bodies receive new life and begin to function in perfect and permanent fashion. As a sample of how this will be we have only to look at Mary. He has already given this gift to his Mother. She lives in heaven, body and soul.

The Final Judgment

At that time, too, Jesus will pronounce final judgment on everyone. Then we will know how God's plan for man worked out in the life of everyone. Then, the people who accepted God and followed him in their lives, responding to the best of their ability to what he asked of them, will enter their Father's house forever. The others who rejected him and refused to follow his path and turned down his demands on them, will be free to follow the life they have freely chosen. They will be left to themselves as they wished, but they will live forever separated from God and the happiness that life with him brings.

- READING FROM JN. 5:19-30.

We call these two lives heaven and hell. Heaven is the life of perfect union with God shared by those who have accepted their Lord and Savior. It is a total sharing of all that God has and is. Since God is full and perfect life, this means total happiness, because this is what men were meant to have when God created them. Heaven is our true home, and it will never be taken away. It is hard to describe because there is nothing like it anywhere. All we can do is imagine all of the happiness that is possible and multiply this a thousand times over. This would still be only the merest hint of what heaven is really like.

Hell, on the other hand, is the opposite. It is misery and isolation. Men were meant for God. When they refuse to accept him they cannot find happiness anywhere else. So hell is a life of hatred and resentment and misery. No one goes to hell who does not choose it. God would rather everyone came to him and received his life, but men are free. He will not force them against their will. So there is a hell and it is very real. It lasts forever. It is a great mystery why anyone should choose this fate, but it is part of the mystery of human freedom. If there wasn't a hell, man wouldn't really be free. He wouldn't have any real choice. He would have to do what God wanted. The possibility of hell guarantees man's freedom.

When will the coming of Christ take place?

- READING FROM MK. 13:32-37.

While no one knows exactly when it is going to happen, Jesus has given us certain indications that will tell us that he is coming.

- READING FROM MK. 13:3-27.

The language of Jesus here is difficult for us because it is from the Old Testament. The apostles and his other Jewish listeners understood it better than we do. They had been brought up on it. What it boils down to is this: first, there will come terrible persecutions. This is not unusual in the history of the Church, since there have been bloody persecutions in the past and there are some going on right now in Iron Curtain countries. But apparently this will be the worst of all. Many Christians will lose their lives. There will be great fear, and lots of people will abandon their faith. Next, there will come a person who will try to set himself up in the place of God. He has always been referred to by Christians as the Anti-Christ. He will try to act like God. In the middle of all this, just about the time when it looks as though the Church is going to go down, suddenly there will be strange and tremendous signs in the sky. The sun, moon and stars will change, and there will be great movements of light and power. This is the signal that Christ is coming. Then he will appear in some way that will be evident to all. He will appear in all his glory and power and then will be the resurrection and judgment. World history will be over, and the reign of God will be perfectly established forever.

This much we know from what God has revealed to us. But we won't know when really, until it happens. People get upset about this when they think of the end of things, but it will not be a disaster, except for the persecutions. The world will not be destroyed. It will be fulfilled instead, and it will begin a new kind of existence. Everything will be changed for the better. Man and God will not only be reconciled, but will live together in the same life. There will be no more sickness, death or suffering. There will be no more faith or hope or sacraments either. They won't be necessary. There will be only love and perfect harmony between God and man as man comes to know God as he really is.

This will be the windup of God's plan, and we know that it will be successful. We believe in it now. Then, we will see how it succeeded.

Meanwhile what about the people who are dying everyday? What happens to them between now and then?

What Happens at Death

We really don't know much about death and the hereafter except in a very general way. It is impossible to describe because we have no experience of it. We know it is not the end and we know that life goes on, but in a different way. What happens at death is that a person's soul and body are separated for a time. The body is buried and the soul goes on to its own particular judgment and life with God or life in hell. Time stops at death, so there is no way to figure out how long all of this takes and what it is like to live without a body. These are minor mysteries about God's plan which will be cleared up as we live through them.

Purgatory is another one of them. We don't know much about this either. The best thing to say about it is that it is a process of purification which a soul goes through who has done a lot of selfish things in life and hasn't worked too hard to grow in the love of God and neighbor. Many people we know are pretty good, but they need a lot of improvement. If they don't work hard with God in this life, God works hard on them in the next. He helps them get rid of all the selfishness and other obstacles that might prevent them from enjoying life with him. There is no time in Purgatory, so we don't know how it works out. But we do know that it is only a stage that some people pass through in their passage to heaven and the presence of God forever.

A Sacrament for the Sick

There is a special sign of assurance and help that God gives us when death comes near or when sickness and suffering become severe. Jesus spent much of his time healing the sick. We know that one of the main reasons he did this was to demonstrate that he could bring life to people. There are still instances where people are cured of severe illnesses in ways that can only be explained by the healing power of God. But Jesus has a special sacrament for all such situations. Through the sacrament of 'extreme unction' (last anointing) or the 'anointing of the sick,' Christ reaches out to the sick and dying of his people and communicates to them in special fashion his life and strength.

This action of Christ is a healing action. Very often it heals the body. But always it heals the spirit. It unites the person who receives it with Jesus in a special way that enables him to face his illness or death with calmness and trust in the saving power of God. It brings him God's forgiveness of his sins, if he is truly repentant.

- READING FROM JAS. 5:14-16.

Thus, in our own personal history of salvation, there is a special event of God that helps us through a critical stage of our journey. God intervened many times to strengthen the faith of the Israelites on their journey through the desert. He made it possible for them to continue and to grow stronger through their trials. In the sacrament of the anointing of the sick he does the same thing to the Christian who is troubled and afraid. He gives him his own strength to lean on, assures him of his forgiveness and helps him through his illness or his death.

God's salvation is part of our life from beginning to end, just as it has been part of the history of mankind from beginning to end. God is present to us every step of the way. He constantly crosses our path to find an entry into our life so that we can enter his. Jesus has opened the path for us. His Church proclaims to the world that this is so. The Father draws men to listen. When a man realizes this and approaches Jesus, the Savior takes him to himself and communicates his life to him through his sacraments. A man's life is then tied up with God forever, and henceforth God shares what he has with him and asks that man share what he has with God. This is the life of the Church wherein all men of faith share with one another what God has shared with each as they make their common way to their heavenly home.

Questions for Discussion

What is different in the Christian view of world events?
What is the connection between death and sin?

Why must we wait until the end to experience all that Christ has won for us?

Is it fair of God to let anyone go to hell?

How will life in heaven differ from life on earth?

How does the Gospel help your picture of the end of the world?

How can we call the sacrament of extreme unction a real healing?

Basic Bibliography

Christ and the End of the World, Franz Mussner (University of Notre Dame Press)

Death for a Christian, Stanley B. Marrow, S.J. (Paulist Press Doctrinal Pamphlet Series)

Life after Death, Matthew J. O'Connell, S.J. (Paulist Press Doctrinal Pamphlet Series)

Annointing of the Sick, Joseph E. Krause (Paulist Press Doctrinal Pamphlet Series)

PART II
A PREPARATION FOR BAPTISM

INTRODUCTION

INITIATING THE BELIEVER

Upon completion of the presentation phase, the inquirers will have heard the core of the Gospel. The Church has explained herself, her mission and her faith. The basic media of revelation have been employed and God's grace has assuredly been at work. At this point, some inquirers will undoubtedly come to an affirmative decision about the Church and will express the wish to become Catholics. This presents a new catechetical situation. Henceforth we are dealing with believers. These catechumens have understood and accepted the Christian faith. The objective now is to help them build a strong and intelligent commitment. Along with this central need are practical ones of indoctrination into the customs, discipline and piety of the Church.

Consequently, in this part of the catechumenate both format and content change. The accent is now strongly liturgical. Prayer and a religious atmosphere are very important. Instruction is practical and deals with the details of Christian life. The role of the priest diminishes; henceforth, he simply conducts the liturgy. On the other hand, the role of the catechumen and the lay catechist increases for the concern is to form a Christian layman. The more resources of the parish that can be brought to bear in this part of the catechumenate, the better. Holding these sessions in the presence of a parish congregation is desirable as a means for introducing the catechumen into the parish community. It also enables the parish to have some active part in the Church's mission.

Ideally, this phase of the catechumenate should take place during the Lenten season and culminate in the Easter Vigil. However, the format does not require this and, in some cases, such timing will not be possible.

Basic Format

The material that follows consists of nine units. Each is designed as a weekly session for the period between Septuagesima and Easter. The basic format is the same for all. Each unit consists of three sections: an informal instruction, a liturgical action including homily, and a group discussion. Each of these sections should take about thirty minutes, although in some cases the liturgy will require more time. The three sections—instruction, liturgy, discussion—are unified around a central theme for each unit.

Liturgy

The liturgical action varies. Five of the sessions use a bible service. The other four employ the liturgy of baptism in stages. Material for the bible services is indicated in outline form. There can, of course, be wide variation in the selection of prayers, readings and hymns.

A modified liturgy for the stages of baptism is presented in full, and sample homilies are included for each session. Experience indicates that more adaptation and change in the baptismal liturgy is necessary if it is to be truly meaningful to today's catechumens. However, this is still some time off and our present liturgy is all we have to work with now.

The Instructions

The suggested instructions are in general outline form. They are intended to be filled in by the catechist from his own background and knowledge. They should be given by a layman wherever possible. No specialized background or training is necessary as this material deals with matters that are part of everyday Catholic life and education.

Discussion Period

The discussion period is designed to follow the liturgy and flow from the homily rather than the instruction. The suggested questions are drawn up on this basis. The purpose of the discussion is to relate the material of the homily to the life of the catechumens. Lay catechists can provide the necessary leadership for discussion. If a parish congregation is present at these sessions, additional parishioners may be invited to join the discussion groups. The atmosphere should be as informal as possible so as to encourage maximum participation.

Place

The place where these sessions are held is important. The church is desirable if it is not so large that the group is lost in it. In such a case, the desired atmosphere is impossible and it would be better to meet in a smaller room. A chapel is ideal, where this is available. In any case, what is needed is an atmosphere of prayer and community. Often this will best be found in a smaller meeting room that can be arranged for liturgical action.

Where the previous phase, i.e., the presentation of the Gospel, is held in another parish or center, it is important to prepare the catechumen for baptism in his home parish. This is the community of which he is about to become a part, and the more they see of each other the better.

Baptized Catechumens

Those catechumens who have been validly baptized need this period of preparation even though they do not require baptism. Several courses are open for their participation in the baptismal liturgy. Inasmuch as many Protestant baptisms employ a much simpler liturgy, there is no reason why catechumens with such a background cannot fully participate in every stage of baptism save the final one. This would be akin to "supplying ceremonies" as is done in the case of emergency baptism. There is a rich formational value in the use of sacramentals that should not be overlooked. Catechumens who have already experienced the full baptismal liturgy can attend the sessions as part of the Christian congregation and participate through prayer and song.

For the final stage, it might be more meaningful to receive the baptized catechumens on Holy Thursday, instead of at the Easter Vigil. They can make a profession of faith and then receive their first communion in the Holy Thursday liturgy. Later, in the Easter Vigil service, they can renew their baptismal promises along with the rest of the congregation.

Many variations can be introduced into this phase of the catechumenate. Meaningful prayers and para-liturgical actions can surely be created. What follows is in line with the traditional bible vigil and baptismal liturgy. These already have a place in parish life and offer the best point of departure for other forms. This kind of liturgical action and prayer are the heart of the catechumenate and new forms must take shape around them.

FIRST WEEK: FAITH

INSTRUCTION OUTLINE
THE SPIRIT OF PRAYER AND WORSHIP

Introduction

Religion is the sum total of man's relationships with God.

Everyone has a relationship with God, even atheists.

The believer consciously tries to work out this relationship in his life.

The believer's life is generally slanted toward God.

There are particular moments when it is emphasized.

This is prayer and worship.

What Prayer Is

So many people think of prayer as "saying prayers"—it isn't.

That is only one of many ways a man prays; and not the most important.

Prayer is communication with God—verbal, mental, spiritual.

It is the way in which man communicates his hopes and needs, his gratitude and wonder, his sorrow and shame, his love.

Prayer is mostly a recognition of God's presence and love for us.

It is the simplest way by which man lets God into his life.

It is the heart of all religion.

What Worship Is

Worship is more than religious ceremony.

It is man's way of showing God his awareness of God's superiority.

Prayer is man's response to God's presence; worship is man's response to God's importance.

In worship, man acknowledges God's lordship over him and gratefully accepts his dependence.

It is a graceful and sincere acceptance of the facts of life.

God is all and we are completely dependent upon him.

Worship makes this fact a regular part of our life.

106

Spirit of Prayer

What is said or done in prayer and worship is not so important. More important is the spirit in which man prays and worships.

As he comes to know God he is struck by God's goodness and his own sinfulness.

If he is honest, he faces both and follows through on what this implies.

He acts toward God with reverence, love, gratitude, and obedience.

He accepts his own limitations, admits his guilt, and looks to God for help.

In this way he naturally develops a spirit of true prayer and worship that comes alive in every important moment of his day.

Everything a man does then becomes material for prayer and can be shared with God.

Christian Prayer

Christ's life is the best showing of the spirit of prayer and worship.

Everything he said, thought and did he turned toward his Father.

The Christian, united to Christ by baptism, can add his thoughts, words, deeds to this and share in Christ's prayer and worship.

He does this formally at Mass, together with all the other members of Christ.

He does it informally in everything else he shares with Christ.

The true Christian spirit is that of Christ: sharing his loving attitudes toward the Father.

Practice of Prayer

The spirit of prayer is always operating in the Christian's heart.

The Christian prays in words when he wants to pray with others, or when he can't think of anything or when the Church prayers express his thoughts.

He prays for himself, for his family, friends, enemies, the Church, the country and all men.

He brings them by his prayer into the presence and love of God and commends them to his care.

By prayer, he deepens his love for God and man and grows in the likeness of Christ.

LITURGICAL ACTION

FIRST STAGE OF BAPTISM: ENTRANCE INTO THE CATECHUMENATE

Entrance of the Candidates

The candidates assemble in the rear and process to their places led by the priest, vested in a surplus and a purple stole, and a lay lector. The community stands in place in the hall or church. During the procession the candidates recite or sing Psalm 41 (or appropriate hymn).

When the psalm is ended the priest faces the community and begins the service. All respond.

Priest: O God come to my assistance.

All: O Lord make haste to help me.

Priest: Glory be to the Father, and to the Son, and to the Holy Spirit.

All: As it was in the beginning, is now, and ever shall be, world without end. Amen.

Priest: Lord have mercy.

All: Christ have mercy.

Priest: Lord have mercy.

Let us pray. Grant O Lord that your catechumens, when they have been taught by these holy mysteries and renewed at the font of baptism, may be numbered among the members of your Church, through our Lord.

All: Amen.

The Request for Faith

The request for faith is preceded by an instruction from scripture read by the lector. All sit.

Lector: The candidates before us are taking the first step toward living a full life of faith. St. Peter tells us about the sublime dignity and privilege of this life to which Jesus, out of his mercy, calls us. He reminds us of the earthly trials we must face, and he encourages us with the thought of the complete and indescribable joy which will be our reward. The lesson is from First Peter, chapter one.

SCRIPTURE READING: 1 Pet. 1:3-12.

The community responds to the Word of God by reciting or singing Psalm 22.

Priest: Will those seeking entrance into the catechumenate of the Church please stand.

The priest leaves the lectern and comes before each candidate in turn, asking:

Priest: By what Christian name do you wish to be called?

Candidate: ———— (If the person does not have a Christian name, he should add one to his common name in response to the question; e.g., Buster *Thomas.*)

Priest: N, what do you ask of the Church of God?

Candidate: The faith.

Priest: What does the faith offer you?

Candidate: Eternal life.

After each has been questioned, the priest faces the candidates and addresses them:

Priest: If you wish to enter into eternal life, heed the words of Christ and keep the commandments. "Thou shalt love the Lord thy God with thy whole heart, and with thy whole soul, and with thy whole mind. This is the first commandment. And the second is like it: Thou shalt love thy neighbor as thyself." (Mt. 22:37-39) Remember likewise the words of Christ to his Father: "Now this is everlasting life, that they may know thee, the only true God, and him whom thou hast sent, Jesus Christ." (Jn. 17:3)

Signing the Candidates with the Cross

The lector begins by reading a lesson from scripture.

Lector: In a few moments the catechumens will be marked with the sign of Christ, the cross. This will signify that the catechumens will belong to Jesus Christ and will come under his special protection. A Christian is one who gives himself totally to Christ and therefore lives his life for and with Christ. Living with Christ means taking up his cross and embracing his commandments in order to share more fully in his holiness. The Word of God in the Epistle to the Hebrews urges us to be firm in choosing the right path and following Christ in our lives. The lesson is from the twelfth chapter of St. Paul's Epistle to the Hebrews.

SCRIPTURE READING: Heb. 12:1-15.

The community responds by reciting or singing Psalm 120.

After the psalm, the priest comes forward and, facing the candidates, asks:

Priest: Will the candidates for the catechumenate please kneel.

The priest goes to each candidate in turn and traces the sign of the cross on the forehead of each. He says:

Priest: Receive the sign of the cross on your forehead and be a follower of Christ.

When each has been signed, the priest goes to the middle and prays over all:

Priest: Do not be ashamed of Christ's cross, for he did not hesitate to take it upon himself for all of us. Remember, too, the words of Christ: "If anyone wishes to come after me, let him deny himself, and take up his cross and follow me." (Mt. 16:24) Worship God the Father by joining yourself to Jesus Christ crucified.

All: Amen.

Priest: Let us pray. We beg you Lord, kindly hear our prayer and guard these catechumens (N & N) with your unfailing protection. They have been signed by the imprint of your cross; may they deserve, by the keeping of your commandments, to achieve the glory of regeneration. Through Christ Our Lord.

All: Amen.

The community responds by reciting or singing Psalm 99.

The Imposition of Hands

The priest returns to the lectern for a reading.

Priest: The candidates who have come to us have been initiated into the catechumenate. This catechumenate is a preparation for life in the Church. After the lesson from the Gospel of St. John, we, as the Christian community, with the symbolic gesture of the imposition of hands, will warmly claim and accept these catechumens as friends. The Gospel reminds us of what it means to be a Christian. Our obedience to Christ and to his Church is not to be the servile obedience of a servant to his master, for we are not called to be the servants of Christ. We are called to be his friends. Our response should be motivated by love. But this love which binds us to Christ must also bind us to our fellow Christians, and to all men. This Word of God comes to us from the fifteenth chapter of St. John's Gospel. Please stand.

SCRIPTURE READING: Jn. 15:12-17

Priest: Will the catechumens please kneel to receive the imposition of hands.

The priest goes to each catechumen in turn, placing his hands on their heads and saying:

Priest: Through the imposition of my hands receive the Holy Spirit and the blessing of God.

Following the priest, the lector and the sponsors proceed down the line clasping both hands of each catechumen and saying:

Lector and Sponsors: Welcome to the Catholic community.

When the catechumens have been greeted, the lector and sponsors gather around the priest who extends his right hand over the catechumens.

Priest: Almighty and eternal God, Father of Our Lord Jesus Christ, look kindly on these your friends (N & N) whom you have been good enough to call to the beginning of faith. Expel all blindness from their hearts; break the bonds of Satan by which they have been bound; open to them, Lord, the door of your mercy, so they may hasten to the grace of your baptism. Through the same Christ Our Lord.

All: Amen.

Blessing and Presentation of Salt (optional)

The sponsors return to their places and the lector goes to the lectern.

Lector: In just a moment the priest will go to the table to bless the salt. Salt is a part of God's creation. It is something all of us have used and tasted. We use it to preserve and season food. The priest will present a few grains of blessed salt on a piece of bread to each of the catechumens. This symbolic action is meant to convey our prayer and hope that they will be preserved from evil, that they will have a foretaste of the bread of life, and that they will be prepared to profit from the grace of baptism.

The priest goes to the table on which the bread and salt have been set out. He is assisted if necessary by the lector.

Priest: Almighty God, bless this salt which you created with your heavenly blessing in the name of Our Lord Jesus Christ and by the power of the Holy Spirit, that it may drive away the enemy, that you may sanctify by sanctifying, and bless by blessing, in the name of Our Lord Jesus Christ.

The catechumens stand. The priest goes to each of them in turn, touching a piece of bread to the salt and placing it on their tongues.

Priest: Receive the salt of wisdom. May it preserve you for eternal life.

Catechumen: Amen.

Priest: Peace be with you.

Catechumen: And with your spirit.

When he has finished, the priest returns to the center and faces the catechumens.

Priest: Let us pray. God of our fathers, God the source of universal truth, in your goodness look kindly on your friends (N & N) who have tasted this first food of salt. Do not allow them to hunger any more. May they burn with your spirit, rejoice with your hope and always serve your name. Lead them Lord, we beg you, to the cleansing flood of regeneration, that with your faithful followers they may deserve to attain the eternal reward of your promises. Through Christ Our Lord.

All: Amen.

Homily and Blessing

The priest delivers a brief homily. When he is done, he stands in the center and makes a sign of the cross during each of the five blessings. All stand.

Priest: I bless your ears that you might hear the divine commands. I bless your eyes that you might see the brightness of God. I bless your nostrils that you might sense the sweetness of Christ. I bless your mouth that you may speak words of life. I bless your hearts that you might believe in God.

The priest pauses while all kneel. He makes three signs of the cross for the final blessing.

Priest: I bless all of you in the name of the Father, and of the Son, and of the Holy Spirit, that you may enter life eternal and so live forever.

All: Amen.

Priest: The Lord be with you.

All: And with your Spirit.

Priest: Go in peace.

All: Thanks be to God.

Closing hymn.

THE CHRISTIAN VOCATION

It is fascinating to observe the things men really live by. Each person usually displays some predominant quality which colors his whole existence. One man lives mainly in his fears, another lives dishonestly by his wits, while a third is characterized by utter integrity. Centuries ago, St. Paul defined that element which should pervade the life of Christ's followers. "The just man," he asserted, "lives by faith."

Quite likely, everyone here enjoys some measure of this faith. This is especially true of those already baptized. But others, too, have felt the attraction of Christ, prayed for faith, and in quiet ways have responded to God's Word and inspirations. Your persevering attendance, your personal application and moral striving have assuredly won for you some degree of initial faith.

It is baptism, however, which brings this rudimentary faith to vigorous strength and enrichment. Baptism is rightly called the sacrament of faith. At baptism, you make a solemn profession of faith, and declare publicly your heartfelt commitment to Christ. Then Christ in his Church accepts you for his own, making you one of his "faithful." You then have the "run of the house" enjoying the entire heritage of God's new people.

The symbolic baptismal rites we now begin to celebrate will express all this vividly. In addition, these rites will enable you to respond actively and progressively to the personal call initiated by Christ. And since faith is the foundation of all we are doing, I'd like to discuss with you tonight that living faith which baptism perfects in you.

First, your faith should be *enlightened.* You should know what faith is, what it does and what it entails. For our present purposes, it is essential that you realize that faith is the root of everthing in the Christian life. It is by faith that we recognize and accept Christ's word. We perceive, at least in some measure, God's loving plan to save us, to re-make us, and to establish a new creation. By faith, we know that God is our loving Father who wants our love in return, that Christ is our Savior and that his Holy Spirit works in us and in the Church to build up the Body of Christ to its full growth.

God in his mercy has revealed himself and his designs for us.

We could never discover these realities by ourselves, nor appreciate them even after they were revealed, without God's help. When his Word comes to us we receive grace to discern it for what it is. And when those of good heart freely choose to go all the way with Christ, they are baptized. It is then that they receive, among many other gifts, the abiding power of faith. This enables them to understand God and his will for them. And the remainder of their days on earth (and their happiness in heaven) will simply be a gradual living-out of this germ of faith.

Some Catholics brought up in an older school may be inclined to regard faith merely as an intellectual assent to the truths of Christian revelation. Of course, faith is an assent of the mind. But it is very much more than this.

God in Christ gives himself to you. So your response in faith should include all that you are: your mind, heart, will and emotions. The knowledge which faith brings us is highly personal. During these past weeks the Church has simply attempted to help you meet Christ, personally. That is why we have increasingly employed terms like "encounter," "trust," "conversion of heart," "commitment." When Christ challenged men to repent (that is, to change their minds, lives and outlook) and to believe the Gospel, he primarily demanded faith in himself. His message was inseparable from his person. So it is today. In coming to baptism you do assent to Christ's teaching and consent to live the kind of life he lived. But above all else, you make a personal commitment to the person of our Lord. Henceforth, in faith, you take your stand irrevocably with him.

Secondly, through union with Christ in his Church, you should strive to make your faith *firm*. You know that your attachment to your wife or friends can grow or diminish. So with your dedication to our Lord. The faith which comes in baptism is a living reality, not something static. And it should develop in vital stability and firmness through all the experiences of life. Faith, like life itself, can be vigorous, anemic, or near to death—depending upon how we exercise it. You don't lose faith like you lose your car keys; but faith can suffer atrophy from sheer neglect.

The New Testament frequently speaks of the quality of men's faith. It often describes the unbelief of Christ's enemies, and the robust faith of people like Mary, his Mother. But it also describes an intermediate state between the total darkness of unbelief and that of ardent faith. Once the father of a deeply-troubled boy begged Christ to cure his son. Christ then asked the father if he was a believer, and the man replied, "Lord, I believe, help my unbelief." This anguished father was saying, in effect, "Lord, you know that, in my heart of hearts, I trust you sincerely. But my frailty often holds me back from perfect discipleship. Help me make my faith stronger." Many of us will recognize in ourselves a striking likeness to this father. We believe, but not as firmly as we would like. So that now, and even after baptism, we should often pray: "Lord, I believe, help my unbelief."

We live in a period when it is nearly impossible to live by a superficial, nominal faith. The world we enter daily, in its opinions, customs, and goals does not always support the Christian outlook. Events in the world, and in the Church reforming herself, confront us with increasing challenges to faith. I prefer to regard all these tests as opportunities rather than dangers. A basically healthy faith, if nourished by persevering prayer, study, and reflection will emerge stronger and more mature than before. Christ is ever calling his disciples to a purer, more interior, and firmer faith. He will never allow you to be crushed or overwhelmed, providing you keep your part of the covenant he makes with you in baptism.

Closely allied to all this, yet deserving of special mention, is a third quality of living faith: it should be *practical*. An enlightened faith which grows increasingly firm, entails specific consequences in our daily lives. "Be ye doers of the word, not hearers only, deceiving yourselves," says the apostle James. And Christ himself couldn't possibly be clearer: "I have given you an example, that as I have done, so do you also."

It is only too obvious that there are some who practice Christianity, but only when it is convenient. They reject no article of the Christian creed and they appear to be devout. But they draw the line in their practice of faith where it conflicts with their selfishness, prejudices, or obstinacy. I am not referring to those who sin through weakness, perhaps often and outrageously, but who are quickly repentant. Nor do I have in mind those troubled in conscience by problems on which Catholic teaching may not be completely clear in its specific application.

A practical faith is one which makes a loving response to God by observing the commandments, applying the beatitudes, and by obedience to those personal inspirations the Holy Spirit stirs in each of us. From the time of Abraham down to this moment, God calls us and expects our union with him to be manifested in our actions. No one ever does all this perfectly. Even the saints had their off-moments. That's why Christ gave us the sacrament of penance for sins committed after baptism.

There is a reciprocal relationship between faith and Christian virtue. Living faith, we have said, should show forth in all the actions of the day. But notice this, it frequently happens that as soon as a man begins to live Christ's ideals, he then comes to a clearer understanding of Christ and his message. Our Lord once advised that if his hearers would only do God's will, they would soon see that he was from the Father, and would then welcome and believe in him.

Your initiation into the Church now takes on a more religious, sacramental character. You will continue to learn; but we trust you will, in public prayer, enter more fully into the mystery of Christ. In all likelihood you will win deeper insight into areas of your life that could be more worthy of a disciple of Christ. And if, each day, you try to serve Christ's ideals, you will advance toward that living faith which transformed people like yourselves into saints and martyrs.

Questions for Discussion

What is the heart of Christian faith?

How can this faith enter every part of a person's life?

What helps faith to grow?

If a person must believe before he is baptized, what does baptism add to his belief?

What changes in his life can faith effect in a person?

SECOND WEEK: CHARITY

Introduction

The idea of commandments and obligations sometimes holds people away from God.

Christianity is not a series of legal restrictions; nor is it a collection of virtues.

It is God's complete gift of himself and his way of life to man.

Within this gift are the good things that come out of a man who has entered the life of God.

What Morality Is

Entering the life of God brings about certain changes in a person.

"Morality" is the Christian's adjustment of his actions so that they will show what has happened to him.

God—Father, Son and Holy Spirit—has taken up residence in him in the closest personal way.

God's life is shared with the Christian so that he now acts as God acts.

God lives by a kind of law—love—and he brings his way of love with him into the life of the Christian.

The Christian's full participation in God's life of love means that he too has a law of love.

The Christian joyfully accepts this way of life because his law is not a rule but a person whom he loves.

Christian morality is not a burden but a gift that fills man's selfish actions with the loving life of God.

Commandments

The commandments are explanations in words of how the love of God is expressed in human actions.

They are guides that make it easy for the Christian to understand where God's love is pushing him.

Through his Church, God teaches man in this way what the inner sharing of God's life is doing to him.

The commandments show how the life of God grows in him and how it is held back.

He obeys not the commandments but the inner love of God they describe.

As a Christian grows in the life of God these external guides no longer have as much importance.

He does naturally and lovingly in every action of his life those things that best express God's life within him.

He does this because he thinks like God and wants the same things God wants.

A Composite Gift

God has given us only one gift—himself.

However, that gift has many sides; morality is only one.

It makes no sense when taken out of the package by itself.

Other sides of the gift are God's continual self-giving in the sacraments, especially the eucharist.

This continual encounter with God enlarges our sharing in his life, and molds our life to him.

In this way we become "good" and more like God.

Prayer and reading of scripture are other ways we encounter God.

So they, too, are sources of Christian moral life.

Christ, Our Model

In Christ as a human being we see the perfect Christian life.

God was completely in him and expressed himself completely through him.

Joined to Christ in baptism, we not only imitate his life, but live it by the same Spirit whom God has given us.

We, too, become sons of God.

LITURGICAL ACTION
BIBLE SERVICE

1. Entrance hymn or psalm.

2. First reading: Eph. 4:17—5:2.

3. First homily.

4. Response to the Word of God: (alternating from side to side)
   a. Beloved, let us love one another for love is from God.
   b. He who does not love God does not know God; for God is love.

   a. There is no fear in love; but perfect love casts out fear.
   b. Let us therefore love, because God loved us.

   a. If anyone says, "I love God," and hates his brother, he is a liar.
   b. In this we have come to know his love, that he laid down his life for us; and we ought to lay down our life for our brothers.

   a. Glory be to the Father . . .
   b. As it was in the beginning . . .

5. Hymn or psalm.

6. Second reading: Jn. 15:9-17.

7. Second homily.

8. Response to the Word of God: (alternating from side to side)
   a. As the Father has loved me, I also have loved you. Abide in my love.
   b. Come, Holy Spirit, fill our hearts with your love.

   a. If anyone love me, he will keep my word, and my Father will love him, and we will come to him and make our abode with him.
   b. Come, Holy Spirit, fill our hearts with your love.

   a. Greater love than this no one has, that he lay down his life for his friends.
   b. Come, Holy Spirit, fill our hearts with your love.

   a. Glory be to the Father . . .
   b. As it was in the beginning . . .

9. Closing hymn or psalm

THE HOLY SPIRIT AND THE LAW OF LOVE

What does it mean to be good? Unhappily, for some Christians it seems to mean keeping a few commandments, obeying a few laws. This is the price we pay for heaven. God gives us these commandments to test our loyalty. If we pass the test, we'll be rewarded forever; otherwise, we'll be punished.

How different a view of the good life is that presented in the New Testament reading. "Be you imitators of God, as very dear children, and walk in love, as Christ also loved us." Goodness, in a word, is being like God, it is Godliness. And we have the flesh-and-blood example of what God is like in Jesus who throughout his life acted always out of love, love for his Father, love for us.

Nothing is more important for you than seeing from the very beginning the relationship between faith and morality, between membership in the Church and your daily life. For unless we see morality, not as keeping commandments and avoiding evil, but as loving our heavenly Father and our neighbor as Jesus did, then the practice of our religion can become quite uninspiring to others and more of a burden than a joy to ourselves.

St. Paul lists by name various kinds of evil which Christians are to avoid: lying, sinful anger, stealing, cursing, revenge. But why are these wrong, why are they not in keeping with a Christian life? Is it because there are commandments against them, because God punishes conduct of this kind? No, rather because for us to do evil makes us living contradictions, it goes against who we are, who we become by baptism—children of God, brothers and sisters of Christ.

We are children of God, and like father, like son! God is our Father, we know, not merely because he gave us human life but especially because he causes us to be re-born by baptism into God's own life, the family life of the Holy Trinity. And what is God's life, what is the distinctive family trait of the Father, the Son, and the Holy Spirit which they share with us? The bible says simply: God is love. This is the closest we can come to expressing what God is like: love.

But love is such a common word, we use it almost without thinking. So we turn to the record of God's deeds to show us what it means to say: God is love. For no other reason than that he wanted to share his happiness with us, God created us. This then is love—self-giving, sharing, generosity. For no other reason than that he wanted to rescue us from human weakness, the Father sent his Son as our Savior. This is love—compassion, sympathy, mercy. After becoming one of us, God's Son went about doing good and finally gave his life for all men. This again is love—the service of others, self-sacrifice.

No wonder then St. Paul, telling us to imitate God, offers love as the reason for doing good and avoiding evil. Don't lie, he says, because we are members of one another. Don't steal but make an honest living so you have something to give others. Speak in a way that will help, not harm, those who hear you. Away with bitterness and malice; on the contrary, be kind to one another and merciful, generously forgiving one another. And notice again why: because "God in Christ has generously forgiven you."

So what does it mean to be good? It means to be like God. It means to be true to ourselves, not to our weak human selfish selves, but to the new selves we become by baptism. A Christian is a child of God in the likeness of God's Son Jesus. "God ordained that we should be shaped to the likeness of his Son," we read in the Epistle to the Romans. Christian conduct therefore is the imitation of Christ.

Goodness is the generous giving of ourselves to our life-task as Jesus gave himself to his vocation. "I do always the things that please the Father," he said. Morality is loving others, showing our love in countless practical ways to all men. "For if God has so loved us," says holy scripture, "we in turn are bound to love one another."

True (we will speak of this later) we sometimes need commandments and laws to remind us what love means, but there is a vast difference between the man who obeys God because he has to and the man who, as a loving son, does everything he can to please the Father. The first does less but finds it harder; the second does more but finds it easier.

Love is always stronger than fear, and the very same love which moved God to create and redeem us is given to us when we become Christians, members of God's family. More and more we should allow this love to guide and influence our daily lives.

THE WILL OF THE FATHER

If a child as he grows up experiences little or no love from his parents and those around him, he will be stunted for life. Never having received love, he will find it hard to give. Faced with the laws of society and the demands of adult life, he will rebel. Why should he do anything for anybody else, since—as far as he knows —no one has ever done anything for him? We are made to be loved, and anyone who has not been loved is bound to be selfish, to look out only for himself.

The glorious truth which Jesus reveals to us in this Gospel passage is that we *are* loved, all of us, by our Father in heaven and by Jesus himself. We simply would not exist except that God wanted us, not as a people in general, but as unique individuals. We simply would not have an eternity of happiness waiting for us except that Jesus, God's Son, gave his life for us, for you, for me.

It is upon this revelation of God's love for us that our lives as Christians must be based. God does not expect us to serve him, to keep his commandments just to avoid punishment. No, if this were the case, like the unloved child we would necessarily be selfish and do nothing beyond what we had to do for our own good.

God has taken great care to show that he first loves us. Knowing that we are already loved, with a love far greater than all human love, then we are able to love in return, not as servants or slaves but as friends of Christ and sons of the Father.

But merely knowing that we are loved by God is not enough. Even the child of loving parents can still on occasion be selfish and ungrateful. He can blind himself to what love demands of him, in small ways, even in important matters. He can choose not to respond to what he has received. And we children of God can do the same.

So Jesus, a little later in the discourse we read, promised to send the Holy Spirit into the hearts of all his friends. The Spirit is the love which Jesus and his Father have for one another. We know how two human persons or a human family speak of "our love" as the power which binds them together. Between the Father and the Son, their love is another person, whose very personality is that he is their mutual love.

It was the Holy Spirit who led Jesus to know and do the Father's will while he was on earth. Now this same Spirit lives in us, the brothers and sisters of Christ, to guide and strengthen us to respond to God's love, to be truly Christlike in our daily lives.

It is the Holy Spirit, the Spirit of Jesus, who enlightens our conscience to see not only the most obvious requirements for imitating Christ—what is stated in the ten commandments and the laws of the Church, for example—but to discover how we as individuals are to show our love for God and for all God's children, our fellow men.

To take as our ideal a life that doesn't directly violate particular commandments or laws is almost to make the Holy Spirit a needless companion and guide in our lives. Such a life, we can be sure, will regularly fall short of what Jesus gives as his commandment: that we love one another as he has loved us. Such a life will hardly produce in us that joy which Jesus says is the reason he told us of the Father's love for us. And such a life will scarcely attract others to the Church in the way the lives of the early Christians did, about whom the pagans said: "See how they love one another!"

At times we will all come face-to-face with a serious moral precept. Our Father's saying "no" may be the only word able to reach us, just as a very young child can be reached only by a firm "no" from his parents. But as we develop into mature Christians, love becomes our rule. The servant, Jesus says, does not know what his master does, but we are sons, friends. By listening to the Spirit and trying to see how everything God asks us is in some way the demand of love, we are gradually made more Christ-like. The question we ask ourselves is not "Is this wrong?" but "What would Christ do?"

Questions for Discussion

What does it mean "to be good"?

Is there any point in being good if you don't believe in God?

Does man need God to be able to love?

What makes an act evil?

If love is the heart of morality, why do we need commandments?

THIRD WEEK: CHRISTIAN MARRIAGE

SEXUAL MORALITY

Introduction

Marriage is a community of persons that is both an image of the life of God and a preparation for it.

As an image of God's life, it is based on love—the love of husband and wife.

As a preparation for God's life, it demands the growth in love that only repeated acts of self-giving can bring.

Like God's love it is creative, and children are an expression of love.

The Meaning of Sex

Marriage is the best expression of a total human love; two people give themselves to each other completely.

This gift is expressed in different ways, in words, attitudes and actions.

It is expressed physically by the sexual giving of husband and wife; for marriage is a community of sex, too.

Sexual union is both an expression of love and a way by which love grows.

It is also the human act through which God creates human beings.

It is integral to marriage because it is the most complete way in which the the human body and emotions participate in love and creation.

The Morality of Sex

Sexual union belongs to marriage because only in marriage is there a complete and permanent gift of one person to another.

Only in marriage, then, should the physical expression of love be complete.

Other human relationships do not involve this total giving.

Their physical expression ought to express only as much as the gift involves.

Adultery is wrong because at least one person has already committed himself completely to another.

Pre-marital relations are wrong because the irrevocable gift of one person to another has not yet taken place.

In both cases, sexual union expresses physically something that has not taken place spiritually.

This is a distortion of human life, for the physical is the vehicle of the spiritual in man.

All sexual activity that does not reflect a previous and complete spiritual gift of self (however imperfectly made) by husband and wife is wrong because it denies the basic spiritual character of man.

Birth Control

God's love is creative and he intends within his plan, that man's love should be the same.

To positively exclude the creative possibilities of married love for reasons of his own, is for man to shut off his life from God's.

To harmonize these possibilities within the overall plan of God, as man learns it from the circumstances of life and the teaching of the Church, is for man to take his full and responsible position in that plan.

LITURGICAL ACTION
BIBLE SERVICE

1. Entrance hymn or psalm.

2. Prayer for enlightenment.

Priest: O God, come to my assistance.
All: Lord, make haste to help me.
Priest: Glory be to the Father, and to the Son, and to the Holy Spirit,
All: As it was in the beginning, is now, and ever shall be, world without end. Amen.
Priest: The Lord be with you.
All: And with your spirit.

Priest: Let us pray. Lord our God, your apostle Paul tells us: Love is very patient, very kind. Love knows no jealousy, makes no parade, gives itself no airs, is never rude, never selfish, never irritated, never resentful; love is never glad when others go wrong; love is gladdened by goodness, always slow to expose weakness, always eager to believe the best, always hopeful, always patient. Love never disappears. Help us to learn to live by this Christian love. We ask this through Jesus Christ, your Son and our Lord.

All: Amen.

3. Response and prayer. *The people respond by reciting Psalm 126:1-5. After the psalm, the priest prays as follows:*

Priest: Let us pray. God of love and fidelity, renew your blessing on all who enter marriage. Help them to keep true faith with each other. May they live in peace according to your will. And may they live in mutual love. Through Christ our Lord.

All: Amen.

4. First reading: Tob. 8:4-10.

5. Response to the Word of God:

Priest: Let us kneel and pray. Father Almighty,

All: Grant your grace to all the families of the world.

Priest: Christ of Cana,

All: Bless every marriage feast.

Priest: Christ of Nazareth,

All: Give unity to every home.

Priest: Christ, Savior of all human persons,

All: Help us to see the eternal worth of a child. Help us to respect each other. Help us to share each other's burdens. Help us on our journey to the heavenly marriage feast.

6. Second reading: Eph. 5:21-33.

7. Homily.

8. The people respond to the Word of God.

Priest: Let us kneel and pray. God, Father, Son and Holy Spirit, you created our first parents and joined them in holy union.

All: Sanctify the hearts and bodies of all who marry.

Priest: May God unite their hearts
All: In the lasting bond of pure love.
Priest: May they be blessed in their children,
All: Supporting one another in joy, in sorrow, and in the duties of each day.
Priest: May your merciful forgiveness blot out their forgetfulness, negligences and sins,
All: And may the graces of your sacrament aid them to be worthy of your high hopes for them.
Priest: May God the Father, Christ the Son, and the Holy Spirit of love grant patience, self-sacrifice and generosity to all who marry. May they be a true sign of the love that binds Christ to the Church. May they and their children, at the end of life, arrive safely at their eternal dwelling where there is no sorrow, sin or death, but only God's love everlasting to enjoy.
All: Amen.

9. Closing hymn or psalm.

SUGGESTED HOMILY
CHRIST'S LOVE FOR THE CHURCH

Despite the difficulties which our era of salvation history brings to married Christians, it also brings them extraordinary blessings. On balance, the good effects of God's current interventions immeasurably surpass the evil around us.

List exhaustively the long catalogue of contemporary offenses against sex and the family. Face squarely that purely secular concept of marriage which through social custom exerts so powerful and pervasive a pressure on everyone. And do not, by any means, evade those questions of conscience which so severely try God's elect today. But having done this, you describe only one angle of a larger canvas. God, ever faithful to his covenant, still comes blessing his people—often in unexpected ways.

For one thing, indiscriminate, wholesale censure of "the world" would be unjust considering the valuable insights into the mystery of marriage given us by many non-Christian scholars. God works even outside the boundaries of his Church. The personalist aspect of sex clarified for us by the psychologists, and problems like the population explosion detailed for us by sociologists—these alone make us deeply indebted to many who do not share our religious convictions. Pope Paul acknowledged this when he approved those efforts that brought about "the freer and more discerning choice of a marriage partner, the deeper solicitude for the development of husbands and wives, the more lively interest taken in children's education and the many factors still being studied by specialists." Even outside the Church, the landscape is not completely bleak.

In the Church, we see manifold evidences of the direct action of Christ's Spirit. There is the revival of family piety, the efforts of young people to prepare for marriage, and the various associations of married couples to study, reflect and share their experiences in Christian family living. Articulate lay Catholics, facing the torturing dilemmas to Christian conscience in marriage today, are producing a literature which is unique in Christian history. At its best, this writing is informed, realistic and manifests a yearning for the highest realms of prayer. Sometimes its scholarship is so profound and its insights so rich that no theologian can henceforth ignore it.

Recall, too, the forthright, eloquent awareness of the problems of married couples manifested by leading churchmen at Vatican II, culminating in a special commission by Pope Paul to review our current teaching. Marriage is one of those matters that have compelled us to go more deeply into the wider question of doctrinal development and the teaching authority of the Church.

Be assured that there is gain in all this, not loss. Be patient and I can promise you—not immediate, pre-fabricated and complete answers; but solutions that will preserve the continuity of Christian truth with healthy progress in our understanding and application of it. It is not easy to wait; yet we cannot force God's hand. And be grateful for the tireless study, prayer and consultation that is invested in the solution of these matters while we await greater clarity from God.

Possibly the deepest justification for Christian optimism on the part of those who marry in Christ is the doctrinal renewal which has enriched their understanding of their role within the total mystery of Christ. A galaxy of scholars have enabled us to see more clearly that God's revelation of himself is declared in terms of marriage. In his progressive manifestation of himself, God calls a people, cares for them and binds them to himself in ever-stronger intimacy. But with the prophet Hosea, Yahweh describes this love as being like the union of man and wife. Afterwards, especially in the prophets, the predominant image of God and his chosen people is that of a marital relationship. This deepened Israel's realization of Yahweh's personal and familiar alliance with them. But it also helped to purify Israel's appreciation of marriage. The rich love between spouses which God blessed at the beginning of time, now achieves a new dimension in dignity. The love between man and wife can now be seen as a reflection of the love between Yahweh and the people of his choice.

When Christ came, he identified himself and his divine claim as the bridegroom of the new people of God. He defends his apostles, for example, against the Pharisees on the ground that they have every right to feast and rejoice because the "bridegroom" was with them! And the Last Supper was the fulfillment of those parables which proclaimed the coming of the kingdom as a marriage banquet. Christian theology, liturgy, catechetics and preaching are at one in describing the Church as the bride of Christ. This is not exaggerated rhetoric; it is the literal truth.

This is perhaps best revealed in St. Paul's magnificent portrayal in the fifth chapter of his letter to the Ephesians. A central feature of this evening's assembly is the reading of this treasured passage. St. Paul is addressing converts who live in a city notorious for its desecration of sex and human love. And in this seemingly unpromising setting he proclaims that Christian marriage is an efficacious sign of Christ's marriage to his Body, the Church. Little wonder that Mother Church makes this part of the Liturgy of the Word in the nuptial Mass.

When a Christian man and woman celebrate the sacrament of matrimony, they exercise—and continue throughout their marriage to exercise—the priestly character bestowed on them in baptism and confirmation. The husband causes sanctifying grace for his wife and she for her husband. Second only to the eucharist, their married love—in all its great and small expressions—are occasions when Christ's love for them is symbolized and made actual. All Christian growth is a maturing in Christ's love. Husband and wife develop in Christian personality by the sharing of their love in Christ.

No good purpose is served by being less than frank. When God created man and woman he ordained that sexual intercourse be the embodiment and expression of their mutual love. But when

Christ made marriage a sacrament, he gave higher meaning to this embrace of love, and to all the many evidences of love that unite a couple. He made the act by which they consummate their affection a sign of the union between himself and the Church. So in this union between married Christians, he transforms their embrace into an action of authentic Christian charity or love. Each now loves the other with the love that is in Christ and that is granted to us so richly by the Holy Spirit. Authentic love in marriage, even beyond the frontiers of God's people, can be and often is a noble human experience. But when Christian marriage strives for its best expression, it approaches that community of love by which Father, Son and Holy Spirit are inseparably united.

It is in the light of this vision that we are to see the basic goals and values which the Church has tried to serve during the moral turbulence of two thousand years. Beneath the din of battle against those within or without who, for whatever reason, would lower Christian standards, there is a Christian message that ever grows in clarity. It grows—and there is no point in denying it— even amid the half-lights, gropings, and incompleteness which often characterized Christian teaching during its progressive development.

What are these goals and values? I turn for assistance to a Catholic layman, John Noonan, who spells this out beautifully. "Procreation is good. Procreation of offspring reaches its completion only in their education. Innocent life is sacred, the personal dignity of the spouse is to be respected. Marital love is holy. In these propositions the values of procreation, life, personality, and love are set forth. About these values a wall had been built; the wall could be removed when it became a prison rather than a bulwark."

It is a high privilege for me to proclaim the essential nobility, dignity and sublimity of Christian marriage; and a privilege for the married, in Christ, to experience something of its exalted grandeur. But like much else in the Christian life, marriage is obviously not lived continuously at a peak of exultation. It can have moments of near-ecstasy; but it is more often lived in the commonplace, prosaic events of every day. Men and women marry; angels do not. And the integrity of a good marriage may be most frequently evidenced in the endless duties to provide for and make a happy home; making ends meet; watching over a sick child; being tolerant of shortcomings; facing the storms of life and the shadow of death with mutual generosity. And where a couple are one in prayer, faith and self-sacrifice—Christ is closer to them than they are to themselves.

Questions for Discussion

What are some of the opportunities for Christian witness in marriage?

How does Christ's love become part of marriage?

How can responsible married life help the partners toward Christian maturity?

What makes marriage a vocation from God?

What greater meaning does Christian baptism give to sex?

FOURTH WEEK: THE TEACHING CHURCH

CONSCIENCE AND AUTHORITY

Introduction

The Christian's response to God includes the desire to obey every call God makes upon him.

God speaks to him in many ways and he must learn to listen.

He grows as a person and as a Christian depending upon how alert and responsive he is to God's message.

Conscience is what points to God's will for him in every situation he faces.

Conscience

For a person to be certain in his conscience about a course of action means he is certain this is what God wants of him.

So he must follow the direction laid out for him at all costs.

However, his certainty can be based on a mistake about the facts or some ignorance about God and his ways of acting.

So, a Christian must learn as much as he can about God and his dealings with men so that he will accurately interpret God's calls on him.

A Christian's conscience even tells him that God wants this so that God can communicate with him.

The Teaching Church

Most of what the Christian knows about God and God's general expectations of him, he learns from the Church.

Christ continues to speak through his Church to his people and has guaranteed that he will not mislead them.

He has sent his Spirit into the Church to inspire and guide his people.

The Church believes that God has done this, and that is why Catholics believe the teaching of the Church.

The Office of Teacher

The bishops are the official teachers of the Church for they are the present apostles whom Christ has commanded to teach what he taught.

The pope as bishop of the whole Church is also its teacher.

What the bishops, together with the pope, teach about what God has said and done is the faith of the Church.

Infallibility is the guarantee Christ has given us that the Church's teachers will never go wrong in their official teaching to the whole Church on faith and morals.

Teaching and Conscience

The Christian bases his life on his belief that God has done certain things and spoken a certain message.

He interprets the situations and challenges of his daily life as opportunities to advance in his life with God.

So, in deciding how to act in a given situation he looks to what God has said and done for clues.

Often the path is clear. God has clearly revealed how this situation should be handled.

Sometimes it is confused and the Christian must look deeper into his faith and pray for light.

He looks to the Church, her teaching and her reflection on the implications of God's Word for such situations. Usually this is enough; his conscience now sees more clearly what God expects of him.

Sometimes, the situation is unusual and there is no clear light.

The Christian then commends his act to God, prays for guidance and does what he believes, in the situation, to be what God expects.

Always he acts within the Church, for there is no Christian life apart from the Church.

Always his conscience is guided by faith, and his faith is the faith of the Church.

LITURGICAL ACTION

SECOND STAGE OF BAPTISM: RECEIVING THE SYMBOLS OF FAITH

Introduction

In the first action of the rite, the catechumens became part of the Christian community. In this action they are led into the church for the first time. In the early Christian days, catechumens were given the core of Christian revelation when they were admitted to the church for instruction. This prepared them to commit themselves, mind and heart, to the mysteries of Christ. We continue this practice today in the symbolic action of giving them the treasures of the Church: the Gospel, the creed and the Lord's Prayer.

Admission into the Church

The priest stands before the catechumens and invites them into the church.

Priest: Enter into the Temple of God, for it is here that you will dwell with Christ in a life that never ends.

The catechumens process into the church reciting Psalm 83 or singing an appropriate hymn. They stand in place in the front pews for the following prayers.

Priest: O God come to my assistance.

All: O Lord make haste to help me.

Priest: Glory be to the Father, and to the Son, and to the Holy Spirit.

All: As it was in the beginning, is now, and ever shall be, world without end. Amen.

Priest: Let us pray. O God, Father of our Lord Jesus Christ and our Father, grant to these catechumens the light of your Holy Spirit that they may know and love your sacred mysteries and may conform their lives to the life of your Son, Jesus Christ, who lives and reigns with you in the unity of the Holy Spirit, God forever.

All: Amen.

Instruction of the Assembly

The catechumens sit and the lector introduces the two scripture readings. The first is on the Temple of the Lord, and the second is on the spirit of enlightenment.

Lector: You have entered into the Temple of God, and you have taken your place among his people. There is great meaning in this action. Not only have you been led into the Temple, but after your baptism you will become part of the Temple, for as we hear in God's Word from St. Paul's Epistle to the Ephesians, this is the Temple founded by our Lord, the Church, and the cornerstone is Christ himself.

SCRIPTURE READING: Eph. 2:19-22.

The community responds to the Word by reciting or singing Psalm 67. They remain standing.

Lector: You have entered the Temple, and you will be enlightened by the Holy Spirit. This enlightenment is not a secret, hidden knowledge, open only to the elect. In this passage from the Gospel of St. Matthew we hear our Lord describe his message as being open to all who will listen, to the poor, to those who become like children. It is not a message of deep learning, but of faith.

SCRIPTURE READING: Mt. 11:25-30.

After the reading, the priest delivers a homily.

Reception of the Symbols of Faith

The catechumens come forward and stand at the altar rail. Their sponsors stand behind them. The lector brings a New Testament for each sponsor and returns to his place beside the priest.

Priest: We now ask the delegates of the Church to present to these, our beloved catechumens, the source of true teaching, the Word of God's revelation.

One by one, each sponsor presents a book to his catechumen with the words:

Sponsor: Receive and cherish the Word of God.

Lector: What the evangelists have written, what the apostles have announced, what the Church has preached to all men from the beginning, all these things are contained in one place—in the Apostles' Creed. The sacred words of this creed will now be given to you as a light to illumine the path of your life until the blessed end which the merciful God has destined for you.

Priest: We now ask the delegates of the Church to announce the creed to the catechumens, proclaiming the articles of faith.

The sponsors place their right hands on the shoulders of the catechumens and together recite the Apostles' Creed.

Priest: Christ the Lord proclaimed to us the Gospel of his heavenly Father. He also taught his disciples how they should speak to him in prayer. The day of joy has come on which we hand over to you in his name the sacred words of the Lord's Prayer. We now ask the delegates of the Church to recite the Our Father, proclaiming the manner in which we pray.

With their hands on the shoulders of the catechumens, the spon-sors recite the Lord's Prayer together. After the prayer, the com-munity recites or sings Psalm 26.

Final Prayer and Blessing

Priest: You have received the most holy treasures of the Chris-tian community, words of life and petition. Keep them forever in your hearts. The Word of God is powerful. It will enable you and us, who have given these holy treasures to you, to attain the heav-enly kingdom.

All kneel.

Priest: Let us pray. O God, Father of our Lord Jesus Christ, open the hearts of your beloved catechumens, and likewise the gates of your mercy, that through the water of regeneration which brings about the remission of all sins, they may be one in Christ Jesus, your Son.

All: Amen.

The priest makes the sign of the cross over the community and the catechumens.

Priest: I bless all of you in the name of the Father, and of the Son, and of the Holy Spirit that you may have life eternal and live forever.

All: Amen.

Priest: The Lord be with you.

All: And with your spirit.

Priest: Go in peace.

All: Thanks be to God.

Closing hymn.

SUGGESTED HOMILY

THE COMMUNITY OF FAITH

You will soon be members of the Church. But what *is* this Church? Ever really stop to think? It is far more than this stone building, or the sum total of church buildings around the world. Many people think of the Catholic Church only as a big organiza-tion run by pastors and bishops, as a corporation like General Motors or Standard Oil. But no. What you are preparing to be-come a part of is the mystery of God acting in his people, and leading them by a common life and worship to eternal happiness with him. The Second Vatican Council has given us some wonderful insights about the Church. Let us look at some of them.

First, *the Church is a mystery*. This is the title of the very first chapter of the Council's treatment. The Council wanted to make clear that the Church is not at all the product of human hands, but of divine action. By "mystery" we usually understand something secret, something hidden and unknown. But St. Paul corrects this. The great mystery he speaks about is the wonderful divine plan for our salvation—a plan hidden from all eternity in God, but now revealed, unveiled to us in the words and actions and person of Jesus Christ (cf. Eph. 3:4-5; Col. 2:2-3). He calls Christ *the* mystery of God. And since this divine plan and action given to us in Jesus are being continued and prolonged in the Church, the Church herself *is* the unfolding and presence of this saving mystery in the world. So we must never confuse the Church with mere corporations or human organizations.

In order to bring out just how closely the Church is joined to Christ, the bible uses all sorts of comparisons: bride and bridegroom, sheepfold and shepherd, branches getting their life from the vine. But the most helpful one for us is St. Paul's image of the Church as the *Body of Christ*. Christ is the head, and we are the Body—each of us comparable to a separate and distinct and God-given part, each important to the life and action of the whole. The Church, then, is like a living organism that has inner life and grows and develops.

Every living thing has an inner life. In man we call it the soul. It gives life and energy and vigor to the whole, and to each part. It is very important to realize that in the Church, too, there is a common life that binds us to Christ and to one another. This life comes from the Holy Spirit, whom we call the soul of the Church. This is the same life-giving and energizing Spirit that flooded the humanity of Jesus in his resurrection and glorification. So filled was he, so alive with his new life, that he in turn becomes the source of *our* life of grace, just as the head is often thought of as the center and source of our truly human activity. It is this life of the Spirit that makes us more and more like Jesus, more united to him and to each other. This union is called the "mystical" body of Christ.

Next, we must get clear, once for all, that the *Church is people*. In fact, "Church" means "assembly," the assembly of those called together by God. In the Old Testament it was the Jewish people.

Now, since Christ, it is the new people of God, the Church. The Church is first of all the communion—the togetherness—of all who are joined to Christ and to one another by the Spirit.

With an iceberg, the largest part is underwater, invisible—yet very real. Likewise in the Church. The spiritual union is invisible, and can spread out far beyond the visible boundaries of the Catholic Church. So even though lots of people don't have all the advantages and the fullness of the Church as we do, they are truly related to the Church through grace and the Spirit. On the other hand, the Vatican Council also stresses another point: namely, that *full* incorporation, full communion with the people of God calls for something more than inner and invisible togetherness. It calls for belief in the same doctrines, worship through the same sacraments, and acceptance of the same God-given guidance of bishops and pope. Why is this? Well, this is a family, a people of God who must be openly and visibly one. Doctrine, sacraments and authority make up the *fullness of means* which Jesus left to his followers—means which he saw as necessary in order to lead people most effectively to eternal life. Now, even though other Churches have some of these means (to a greater or lesser extent, depending on which church it is), only the Catholic Church has them all. For this reason we speak of the Catholic Church as the *one true Church.*

Finally, we are *a pilgrim people,* people still enroute to our final home. We are still very human and self-centered, still very weak and prone to sin in spite of God's work in us. Because God is with his people, the Church is holy and unified; but because we are still sinners, this unity and holiness remains to a great extent a goal still to be achieved. This is why the Church must constantly strive for inner renewal and reform—the very things Pope John XXIII called for at the recent council.

Becoming a Catholic is a wonderful thing. Each of you is offered a full and explicit role in the family of God. But this new status also brings a terrific challenge. We in the Church must be the light of the world, "a sign lifted high above the nations" that will attract and guide men to Christ. God can and does save others outside the visible Church. But all the time he wills to have *one* united family, with one united love and faith and worship.

You are joining the vanguard of men and women in whom God's loving-mercy is being made present in the world. You are joining the visible and Spirit-filled people of God called the Catholic Church. "Veteran" Catholics are themselves coming to a new awareness today of the true beauty and challenge of this vocation. You and we will be helping each other to grow in a fuller appreciation of this great mystery of God's love.

Questions for Discussion

What makes the Church different from all other organizations?
What is it that unites the Church?
How can sinners feel at home in the Church?
What is the common task of the whole Church?
As a member of Christ's Body, how should a Catholic look at other people?

FIFTH WEEK: THE MASS

THE STRUCTURE OF THE MASS

NOTE: *This instruction can be given as part of a Mass demonstration.*

Introduction

All religion must involve prayer and worship.
These are the framework within which man approaches God.
The Mass is the most important Catholic act of worship.
It is the people of God assembled to give glory to him.

What the Mass Is

Basically, the Mass is a meeting between God and his people.
When people meet, they speak and act.
In our meeting with God, we speak with him and do something.
At Mass, God and his people exchange *words* and then, *gifts*.

The Words

These words contain truth: God's thoughts and our thoughts.
Our thoughts are expressed in the form of prayers.
God's thoughts are expressed in the bible through which he speaks to us.
The conversation is orderly: first, we speak; then we stop and listen to God.
Thus, the first part of the Mass is a conversation with God.
We confess our unworthiness and ask his pardon (Confiteor).
We sing his praises and ask his mercy (Introit, Kyrie, Gloria).
We ask his love and help (Collect).
God speaks his truth and love (Epistle, Gospel).
The Church explains God's message (sermon).
We respond to God's word in the only way man can (Creed: "I believe!").

140

The Gifts

After the exchange of words comes an exchange of gifts.

Our gift to God is made up of many things: our love (Offertory prayers and actions) our wealth (the collection), as much of ourself as possible, and most important—

His own Son, Jesus Christ, who gave himself for all (Consecration through minor elevation).

Christ's gift of himself to his Father is the heart of what we give at Mass.

God's gift to us is also made up of many things: his love, his saving grace and most important—

His own Son, Jesus Christ, who is given to us as food (Holy Communion).

In exchanging these gifts, we talk to God to express what we are doing (Canon prayers).

We ask his help to make us worthy of the gifts he is giving us (Our Father through prayers before Communion).

We thank him and ask his continued help (Post Communion to end).

The Structure of the Mass

These exchanges follow a particular form because that's how they began.

The exchange of words follows the old Jewish synagogue service in which God and his people met and spoke through prayer and scripture.

The exchange of gifts follows the Last Supper when Christ first gave himself in the form of food.

Together, this prayer service and this sacrificial meal make up the Mass.

Summary

It is a meeting between God and his people in which their love for one another is expressed in words and signs.

LITURGICAL ACTION
BIBLE SERVICE

1. Entrance hymn or psalm.

2. First reading: Is. 43:1-8; 44:1-3.

3. First homily.

4. Response to the Word of God: (alternating from side to side)

   a. Give ear, O heavens, while I speak; let the earth listen to the words of my mouth.
   b. May my instruction soak in like the rain, and my discourse permeate like the dew.

   a. For I will sing the Lord's renown; O proclaim the greatness of our God!
   b. The Rock, how faultless are his deeds, how right all his ways.

   a. A faithful God, without deceit, how just and upright he is.
   b. Is he not your Father who created you? Has he not made you and established you?

   a. Think back on the days of old, reflect on the years of age upon age.
   b. Ask your Father and he will inform you; ask your elders and they will tell you.

   a. When the Most High assigned the nations their heritage, when he parcelled out the descendants of Adam,
   b. The Lord's own portion was Jacob, his hereditary share was Israel.

   a. The Lord alone was their leader, no strange God was with him.
   b. He had them ride triumphant over the summits of the land and live off the products of its fields.

   a. Surely, the Lord shall do justice for his people; on his servants he shall have pity.
   b. When he sees their strength failing, and their protected and unprotected alike disappearing.

   a. Give ear, O heavens, when I speak; let the earth listen to the words of my mouth.
   b. May my instruction soak in like the rain, and my discourse permeate like the dew.

5. Psalm of hymn.

6. Second reading: Heb. 9:11-14; 10:4-10.

7. Second homily.

8. Response to the Word of God: (alternating from side to side)

 a. Give thanks to the Lord, for he is good, for his mercy endures forever.
 b. A new song has been heard in the land, a new song from God's family on earth.

 a. It is a song of joy in praise of God our Savior.
 b. For he has chosen us from every continent, and from every tribe and nation.

 a. He has made us citizens and anointed us priests in his kingdom.
 b. All this is the work of the Lamb who was offered and slain for us.

 a. This is the New Covenant of life eternally sealed in his blood.
 b. Give thanks to the Lord, for he is good,

 a. And his mercy endures forever.
 b. Glory be to the Father . . .

 a. As it was in the beginning . . .

9. Closing hymn or psalm.

SUGGESTED FIRST HOMILY
PRIESTHOOD OF THE FAITHFUL

Several years ago a charming movie was produced entitled *Whistle Down the Wind*. In the course of the movie, three small children approach the pastor of their local church and they ask him a very simple question, "What is God like?"

The pastor in the movie scene is taken back by the question. He seeks refuge in an answer which is theologically correct, but which means almost nothing to the children. In his answer, the pastor uses words like "infinite," "eternal," "immutable," and "ultimate". The children listen politely, but entirely without comprehension. Finally one youngster says to the others, "Com'on, let's go. He doesn't know what God is like either."

Sooner or later every child, and for that matter every adult who has retained childlikeness, must ask the same question. What *is* God like?

We too can answer rather glibly that God is an eternal, omnipotent, infinite Being. We feel sure that this answer is perfectly correct. The only trouble with the answer is that it leaves us feeling that we do not understand God much more after we have heard the answer. Another approach is indicated. Perhaps we can find out a little more about God from the sacred scriptures. What has God told us about himself?

The scriptures tell us many things about God. The bible may be described as a collection of books which tell us about God. Perhaps the passage that is most significant to me is the one found in the Good News according to St. John where it is said that God is a loving Father. "If anyone love me, he will keep my word, and my Father will love him, and we will come to him and make our abode with him." (Jn. 14:23-24)

It is difficult, in fact it is impossible for us to fully understand that Being whose very nature is an outpouring of love; but the description of God as a loving Father who wishes to be with his children has great significance for us. We may not know what it means to be infinite, or eternal, or immutable or ultimate, but we have had experience of what it means to love. We find love hard to explain, but few of us would hesitate to say that love is the most important thing in life. Without love, life is empty and without meaning. With love, life is joyous and fulfilling. Love makes all the difference, and God has told us that he loves us so much that he wishes to dwell with us.

Love of parents, love of family, love of friends, love of husband and wife, love of country, of nature, of learning, of beauty, those are the things that give purpose and meaning to human life. In some vague but very real way all of these loves speak to us of the God who has made them; they tell us something of the God who has loved us more than we can imagine.

God, our loving Father has gathered us, his children, into a community, or better still a communion of love. From the very beginning of time God has chosen to dwell in the company of men. Love seeks union, and our loving Father seeks union with men, he abides with you and me in a communion of love.

From the very dawn of human creation, God has made his presence known and felt in human society. It was the profound experience of the people of the Old Testament that God had come to dwell with them. In the dreary days of desert wandering, God led his people as a pillar of cloud by day, as a beacon of fire by night. He lived with them in the Ark of the Covenant. He set up his tent in the midst of their camp. He spoke to them in their laws, he lived with them in exile, he encouraged them in suffering, he rejoiced with them in prosperity. He fought with them in battle, healed them in defeat, he led them to the Promised Land. In a word, he loved them. The one thing that made the Israelites a people was that they held God in common. The Israelites were called a people of God because the presence of God's love bound them together. God spoke to his people and said, "I shall be to you as your God, and you shall be to me as my people." (Jer. 31:33) "And the whole people answered with one voice. We will do all that the Lord has bidden us." (Exod. 24:3-7)

But that was only the beginning of God's fatherly love for men. God promised more. "Behold the days shall come . . . and I will make a new covenant . . ." (Jer. 31:31) This new covenant, a new union of men with God, was instituted by Christ who called together a people made up of Jew and Gentile, uniting them not according to the flesh, but in the Spirit, the Spirit of Love. For those who believe in Jesus Christ, God become man, who are reborn through the living God, (cf. 1 Pet. 1:23) not from the flesh but from water and the Holy Spirit (Jn. 3:5-6), these people are finally established as "a holy nation, a purchased people." *We* are a single people because we are all in communion with God in Christ, and in communion with one another through Christ.

God our loving Father has sent his Son to live with us. The love that we give, the love that we receive, the love that we generate together is the very sign of our union, of our communion with the God who so "loved the world as to give his only begotten Son." (Jn. 3:16)

What is God like? He is something like the love that we share with one another. God is here, among us now, making us one with him and one with each other. We discover what God is like when ". . . we answer with one voice."

SUGGESTED SECOND HOMILY

THE IDEA OF SACRIFICE

If you are like most people today, you do much of your purchasing on credit. Houses, automobiles, refrigerators, and television sets are able to be had for a small down payment and for an additional monthly sum. It seems that we continue to pay for many of these things as long as we live. The down payment is our pledge of good faith, and our monthly installments are a continuing fulfillment of our commitments.

Much of today's business is conducted in a rather impersonal mechanical way. Frequently we don't even know the people with whom we are dealing. It is this impersonal and technical aspect of contemporary life that is often criticized and dubbed as crass commercialism.

If you had lived in ancient times, you would have conducted your business affairs in a very different fashion. Before you entered into any sort of negotiation or contract, you would spend a long time getting to know and trust those with whom you were dealing. Most times you would deal with a relative, because you would feel that he is more worthy of your confidence.

In ancient Israel, when a business negotiation was agreed upon, the parties would confirm their agreement, not by an earnest payment, but by a sacrifice. The parties would choose something of value, an unblemished lamb from the flock, or the first fruits of a new harvest. The sacrificial victim would be prepared, and both parties would share in it. In this way they would pledge their good faith to one another.

The people of God in the Old Testament not only conducted their business affairs in this way, but they dealt with God in a similar fashion. A sacrificial victim was chosen, prepared, and offered to God. Then it was shared by those who wished to express their good faith with God in the sacrificial meal.

It was by means of sacrifice that the covenant of love between God and man was sealed. God promised to be faithful to those people who were privileged to have him dwell among them, and the people promised to be faithful to their God who had so reached out in love. "I shall be to you as your God, and you shall be to me as my people." This is the covenant that God offered to man, a covenant that was sealed in the blood of sacrifice, a sacrifice which pledged continuing fidelity in a community of love.

The sacrifices of the ancient people of God were of small consequence when compared with the sacrifice of the new people of God in the new covenant. We are privileged to contract or to pledge our love to God and to seal this pledge in a sacrifice in which our unblemished Lamb, our first fruits of the human harvest, is Christ. Because Christ is man, the representative of mankind, he stands for all of us. Because he is God He has a value worthy of God himself. But in this case Christ has become flesh and he dwells in our midst. In offering his life, we offer our own as well. He is priest and victim of the sacrifice, we are sharers in his priesthood and in his victimhood. Through Christ and with him and in him the entire people of God present themselves to the Father who transforms them and then shares the victim with us in a sacrificial meal.

We offer this sacrifice as our pledge of good faith, and we offer it over and over again as a continuing pledge of our good faith. This is no impersonal business affair, but rather the sign of a deep love affair between God and man that reaches its high point in the sacrificial meal.

It is in the Mass more than anything else that we meet the Father. As a priestly people who offer themselves in the name of Christ and with his power; as a people whose victimhood is bound in the blood of the Lamb, we worship the Father; as sharers in the common meal we are bound together with Christ and with one another in a common life of love.

We are the people of God, a community of persons who gather together to see, to listen, to share, to love—in a word, to worship the Father in the name of our risen Lord, Jesus Christ, who joins his Life to our own in a communion of the new covenant, a new joining of God with his beloved people. Let us share this bread and drink this cup as worthily as possible until that glorious day when the Lord will come to lead us to eternal union with the Father.

Questions for Discussion

If God is a Father, what should be our attitude toward him?
Why should God's presence bring us happiness?
How can God unite all kinds of people into a loving family?
How do we "give" when we worship God?
What attitudes toward God does the Mass express?

SIXTH WEEK: THE SACRAMENTS

EXAMINATION OF CONSCIENCE

Introduction

Christian life, like all life, is a process of growth.

There is no standing still; if a Christian does not grow in his life with God, that life in him weakens and will eventually die.

God alone is our judge, but from time to time the Christian must evaluate his response to God's love.

This process is called an examination of conscience.

Sometimes he will have to apply correctives.

How to Examine Your Conscience

No particular form is necessary; nor is any special time, except that it is done on every occasion of the sacrament of penance.

Best to examine self regularly, briefly and honestly.

If it becomes a burden or source of anxiety, it should be discontinued or limited to matters that do not produce this effect.

Its purpose should always be kept in mind: the personal examination is meant to be an aid to growth in the love of God and not a trial that is undergone for his sake.

The Christian seeks to be perfect as "his heavenly Father is perfect."

Material for Examination

A person need not search his soul for serious sin; almost always if he is guilty of such sin, the memory will be very much present to him.

Rather he strives to see himself as God sees him, i.e., as he is.

He looks for his good achievements and seeks ways to make them better.

He looks for his lesser failings and omissions and seeks ways to expand his generosity.

General Things to Watch

The Christian reminds himself who he is—a temple in whom God dwells, and someone beloved by God.

He tries to look at everyone and everything from this point of view and measures his relationships with them in this way, to see where he has let other considerations dominate him.

He measures his concern for others, for the Church, for his countrymen, and for the men of other nations.

Particulars

The Christian examines himself in his own particular life-situation.

Thus: he examines his conduct and attitudes toward God to discover how he has held back on his love or trust in him; how he has ignored him for a time; how he has compromised his God-centered ideals.

He examines himself in his family life—how he has been angry or irritable and impatient or ungenerous toward his wife and children or other members of his family. What are Christ's calls to him as a husband and father?

Toward his fellow workers—has he been fair in his dealings and judgments about them? How is he acting as a Christian office manager?

Toward all the others in his life—how am I helping to improve this city I live in?

Conclusion

He looks to see what progress, if any, he has made since his last examination.

He commends his efforts to God and asks him to help him grow more docile to his love.

He makes a simple practical resolve about where he will concentrate his growth until the next examination.

LITURGICAL ACTION
BIBLE SERVICE

1. Entrance hymn or psalm.

2. First reading: Jos. 1:1-9.

3. Response to the Word of God: (alternating from side to side)

   a. Without a leader, Lord, we go astray.
   b. We are like sheep without a shepherd.

   a. Everything seems in darkness, Lord, without you.
   b. We are like sheep without a shepherd.

   a. We are easily led astray.
   b. Without you as our guide, we are lost.

   a. Only when we understand our weakness, will we turn to you for strength.
   b. Do not leave us alone, O Lord.

   a. Track us down in our wandering, sustain us with your power.
   b. Without you, we are like sheep without a shepherd.

   a. Glory be to the Father . . .
   b. As it was in the beginning . . .

4. Psalm or hymn.

5. Second reading: Mt. 28:16-20.

6. Homily.

7. Response to the Word of God: (alternating from side to side)

   a. A new commandment I give you,
   b. That you love one another.

   a. As I have loved you
   b. You also love one another.

   a. By this will all men know that you are my disciples,
   b. If you have love for one another.

   a. My neighbor is a man like myself.
   b. His blessings can also be mine.

a. He is created in God's likeness,
b. Just as I am created in God's likeness.

a. He is a child of the Church,
b. As I am a child of the Church.

a. He is nourished with the sacraments,
b. The sacraments which sustain my life.

a. Whatever I do against my neighbor
b. I do unto Jesus, the Christ.

a. God has chosen my neighbor to be his representative.
b. I cannot be his disciple,

a. If I have no love for my neighbor.
b. I am not a Christian when I have no concern for my neighbor.

a. If I afflict my neighbor, God will afflict me.
b. If I pardon my neighbor, God will pardon me.

a. If I support my neighbor, God will support me.
b. For he has fed us all with his body, he has united us with himself.

a. The Lord is active in our assembly,
b. Together we must praise him with one voice, one action.

a. Glory be to the Father . . .
b. As it was in the beginning . . .

8. Closing hymn or psalm.

SUGGESTED HOMILY
THE ACTIONS OF CHRIST

Even a casual understanding of the history of the world makes us aware that man is a very imperfect creature. For every glorious deed and bright page of man's history there seems to be an inglorious episode, a dark account of the behavior of men.

If this is true of mankind in general, it seems to be true also of our personal lives. A man who is honest with himself, usually recognizes that he is capable both of virtuous behavior, and at the same time that he must account for ignorance, malice and failure.

Man is an enigmatic being, and his self-seeking and searching makes him doubt his own dignity and nobility. Perhaps this mixed appreciation of man makes it difficult for us to accept the fact that God loves us with a faithful, unchanging, merciful and understanding love that knows no limits. The best assurance of the true value of man comes to us from the knowledge that God has loved men from the beginning of time.

More than this, God has so loved the world that he sent his only begotten Son to lift men to a life of perfect happiness within the very life of God himself. The mystery of the Father who has created us, the Son who redeems us, and the Holy Spirit who sanctifies us, is not only the key to the understanding of history, but it helps us to grasp the meaning of the Church as we encounter it in our own lives.

We must remind ourselves over and over again that it is through the Son, in the Spirit, that we are united to God the Father. This union exists now. In a very real, though qualified sense, it is true to say that "you are Christ." For the Church is the mystery, the visible sign which makes present to us the mediation of Jesus and the gifts of the Spirit so that we may truly call ourselves children of the Father, the family or the people of God who speak with one voice, the voice of Christ himself.

God expresses his love by giving men gifts. The gifts he has given us are not material goods; rather they are all, in one way or another, life. By sharing in a common life we, the many become a communion, a fellowship.

The Church is primarily a communion. It is a sharing of holy things, of holy actions. These actions spring from the life that we share in common, the life of Christ. Of course it is true that the Church is a society with certain legal aspects and structures like other human societies. But all of these structures could pass away and the Church would remain, because in its most fundamental sense, the Church is the mystery of that life of common gifts, of common activities where no man stands alone, but constantly gives and receives, loses his separateness and takes his rightful place as a brother among brothers.

The communion that we experience, that we feel at this moment, is the life of God. "Where two or three are gathered together in my name, there am I in the midst of them." (Mt. 18:20) By drawing together in the vital action of Christ, we are shepherded into the life which Christ shares with the Father in the Holy Spirit. The Church is the fulfillment of the prayer of Christ that ". . . all may be one, as you Father in me, and I in you, that they may also be one in us." (Jn. 19:21)

By sharing his work with us, Christ shares his life, and by sharing his life with us, he shares the Trinity with us. The Church, then, is the mystery of fellowship with the Father, the Son and the Spirit. This is our basic and indispensable notion of what it means to be a Christian. It means that within the community of believers with whom we worship, God reveals himself to us as Father; the Son becomes again our redeemer and the Holy Spirit vivifies us internally so that we are able to carry out the work of surrendering ourselves to the eternal Father. At worship we are indeed the Church of Christ.

The Church then is a mystery or a sign which teaches us that Christ is present and active in our midst. And the life of the Church is present in all her actions which extend the saving acts of Christ. These saving activities of Christ are more commonly known as sacraments.

It is hard for us not to think of sacraments as "things," as if they were material gifts that can be possessed and held. But the truth is that sacraments are much more than "things;" they are living actions or activities which we share with the living Christ.

What kind of actions do we share with Christ? Actions of worship. For every sacrament joins us with Christ in an action of self-surrender, the very root of religion, and enables us to enjoy the companionship of God who gives himself to us. Baptism allows us to re-live the death and resurrection of Christ; penance heals deviations from the Christ-life; confirmation and holy orders are deputations to worship. Matrimony signifies the intimate union of Christ with the members of his flock. The eucharist is a sign of our fellowship with the risen Christ. The sacrament of the sick is the union of our suffering with that of Christ in anticipation of our resurrection. Sacraments are not "things" but the precious power to live with Christ. They flow from the very vitality of the Church which is the mystery of Christ's presence among men.

Sacraments as signs are acts of faith of the Church and of the individual within the Church. By "practice" of our faith, by repeated devout sharing of these actions of Christ, we increase the Christ-life in us. Every noble human activity requires a certain amount of repetition in order that we may become adept at the activity. Living the Christ-life is a difficult activity, and we practice this activity by repeating again and again the actions of Christ which merge his life into ours.

Obviously, then, the sacraments demand our full cooperation. We cannot share the actions of Christ, we cannot join with him in giving and receiving gifts from the Father in the Spirit, unless we are deeply involved. Merely to go through the motions of living the sacramental life is to be lacking in that vital faith which makes it possible for the work of Christ to find good soil. God loves us too much to change our lives without our free cooperation.

Finally, reflection on the sacramental life of the Church brings our eternal goal into the present. Every sacrament signifies not only present gifts, but the past and future, too—the passion and death of Christ, and eternal glory. It is in our encounter with the risen Christ that we come to an understanding of the relationship of our present acts with eternal glory. For the act is initiated and carried on by the Christ of glory, who, by means of the sacraments, initiates us into his life of glory.

What a glorious dignity man has. To be loved by God, and to share the life of God in the sacramental, mysterious actions of the Church. Understand your dignity, live the life of the fellowship, enter fully into the vital actions of Christ, and you can make your own the words of St. Paul, "I live, now not I, but Christ lives in me."

Questions for Discussion

How does God deliver his gifts to us?

What does the Christian do in a sacrament?

Why do we need faith to receive sacraments?

Could a man lead a good Christian life without Mass and the sacraments?

Why do we have to repeat acts of worship?

SEVENTH WEEK: FORGIVENESS

Instruction: How to Go to Confession

There is no instruction outline for this session on the practice of confession. The best way to acquaint catechumens with confession procedures is to demonstrate several sample confessions.

With the help of a couple of lay catechists, several demonstration confessions can be carried out. These should illustrate the proper and improper ways for a person to make his confession. Questions and discussion may be permitted during or after the demonstration.

LITURGICAL ACTION
THIRD STAGE OF BAPTISM: LIBERATION FROM THE BONDS OF EVIL

Introduction

St. Paul tells us we must first put off the old sinful man in order to put on Jesus Christ. We continue to experience the pull of evil all through our lives. In this liturgical ceremony, the catechumen will receive a pledge of divine help to overcome the evil in himself. The Church will help, by the prayers and example of the community, to win the final victory over sin through the power of Christ.

Entrance of the Catechumens

The assembly stands while the catechumens process into the church reciting Psalm 117 or singing an appropriate hymn. When they have reached their places, the priest goes to the center of the altar and prays.

Priest: O God, come to my assistance.

All: O Lord, make haste to help me.

Priest: Glory be to the Father, and to the Son, and to the Holy Spirit.

155

All: As it was in the beginning, is now, and ever shall be, world without end. Amen.

Priest: Lord have mercy.

All: Christ have mercy.

Priest: Lord have mercy.

Let us pray. Holy Lord, Almighty Eternal God, you who from the very beginning have willed that man should live forever with you, we earnestly pray that these, your servants, once born according to the flesh as sons of Adam and subjects of the power of evil, may now be born again of water and the Spirit, as sons of God. Behold your Son who became one of us so that through death he might destroy the empire of death, and grant that these servants whom you have called to the sacrament of faith may rise with Christ from the influence of evil and walk in the newness of life, clothed in the white garment of salvation, unto everlasting life, through Our Lord, Jesus Christ. Amen.

Instruction of the Assembly

The assembly sits. The lector introduces and reads the first scripture passage.

Lector: Our Lord often taught that the forces of evil are like a kingdom which attempts to wage war on God. Jesus himself, in his own person, has brought the kingdom of God among men. He is stronger than the dominion of evil in this world. In baptism, Christ destroys Satan's influence over us and establishes the reign of the kingdom of God in us. The first reading tells of the sin of our first parents—a sin which St. Paul says brought death to all men.

Scripture Reading: Gen. 3:1-13.

The community stands and responds to the Word of God by singing or reciting Psalm 50:1-12. They remain standing.

Lector: Throughout his life Our Lord waged war against the devil and won a victory for us by his death and resurrection. In the second reading, St. Matthew describes the irreconcilable conflict between the kingdom of Satan and the kingdom of God.

Scripture Reading: Mt. 12:22-30.

All respond by reciting:

Through Christ we have been called to freedom, the freedom of the sons of God.

No longer must we be subjects of sin or of Satan.

No kingdom divided against itself can stand.

No man can serve two masters: he will hate the one and serve the other.

Any man who is not with Christ is against him, and he who does not gather with him, scatters.

He who loves his neighbor is a son of God, and Christ will remember him on the last day.

The assembly sits. The lector continues with the third reading.

Lector: St. Paul tells us in the third reading that although Christ begins our victory over Satan at baptism, we must extend this victory in the world through the holiness of our lives. Christ sends us the Holy Spirit to insure our triumph over the forces of the devil.

SCRIPTURE READING: Eph. 6:12-20.

After the reading, the priest delivers a homily. When the homily is finished all kneel and recite Psalm 22.

Sealing with the Sign of Christ

The seal of the living God which is to mark the faithful in the last times (Apoc. 7:2-3) is now placed on the heads of the catechumens to protect them from the influence of evil.

Priest: We ask you sponsors, delegates of the Church, to come forward to make the sign of Christ, the cross, on the foreheads of the elect . . . We ask you catechumens to come forward to receive the sign of Christ, the cross.

When they are called, the sponsors come forward to the front of the church and face the congregation. The catechumens come forward and stand facing them. As the priest makes the sign of the cross over the group, the sponsors sign the foreheads of the catechumens.

Priest and Sponsors: In the name of the Father, and of the Son, and of the Holy Spirit. Amen.

Prayer for Liberation from Evil

The sponsors move behind the catechumens. They all face the priest in the center of the altar.

Priest: Let us pray. God of Abraham, God of Isaac, God of Jacob, God who appeared on the Mount of Sinai to Moses your servant and led the children of Israel out of the land of Egypt, appoint for these an angel of your loving kindness to guard them day and night. We beseech you, Lord, that you may be pleased to send your holy angels from heaven to guard these your servants and lead them to the grace of your baptism.

O God, our Father, who are with us and in us, give us the strength to resist the forces of evil that beset us on every side. We acknowledge you and your Son, Jesus Christ, and the Holy Spirit as the source of our goodness and our protection against harm. As we sign these, your catechumens, with the sign of the holy cross, we ask that it be the mark of your constant protection of them, as it is of their dedication to you, through the same Christ Our Lord, who will come to judge the living and the dead, and this age.

Let us pray. O Holy Lord, Almighty Father, Eternal God, source of light and truth, I ask for these your servants your fatherly love, eternal and most just, so that you may be pleased to enlighten them with the light of your understanding. Cleanse and sanctify them. Grant them true knowledge so that they, made fit for the grace of baptism, may retain unwavering hope, true judgment and sacred teaching. Through Our Lord, Jesus Christ. Amen.

Questioning of the Catechumens

The names of all the catechumens are included in the first question. They answer in unison.

Priest: (Name) do you renounce Satan?
Catechumens: I do renounce him.
Priest: And all his works?
Catechumens: I do renounce them.
Priest: And all his enticements?
Catechumens: I do renounce them.

Anointing of the Catechumens

The priest takes the Oil of Catechumens and anoints each on the right arm.

Priest: I anoint you with the oil of salvation in Christ Jesus Our Lord, so that you may have everlasting life. May God give strength to your arm to vanquish the devil and his angels.

Prayer of the Assembly

The catechumens and sponsors return to their places where they remain standing. The priest returns to the middle of the altar.

Priest: Let us pray for our elect, that God and Our Lord Jesus

Christ may open their hearts and the door of mercy, so that, by the regenerative washing which they will receive for the remission of all their sins, they may be found in Christ Jesus Our Lord.

Let us kneel and pray. Almighty, Eternal God, you who always make your Church fruitful with new members, increase the faith and understanding of your elect, that reborn at the font of baptism they may be included among the sons of your adoption. Through Christ Our Lord. Amen.

Therefore, accursed devil, acknowledge your condemnation and pay homage to the living and true God. Pay homage to Jesus Christ, his Son, and to the Holy Spirit, and depart from these servants of God (N. and N.), for Jesus Christ, Our Lord and God, has called them to his holy grace and to the font of baptism. Accursed devil, never dare to desecrate this sign of the holy cross which we have traced upon their foreheads. Through the same Jesus Christ Our Lord, who is to come to judge the living and the dead and the world by fire. Amen.

Final Blessing

The priest makes three signs of the cross over the catechumens.

Priest: I bless all of you in the name of the Father, and of the Son, and of the Holy Spirit, that you may have life eternal and may live forever.

All: Amen.

Priest: The Lord be with you.

All: And with your spirit.

Priest: Go in peace.

All: Thanks be to God.

Closing hymn.

SUGGESTED HOMILY
LIBERATION FROM SIN

Christian life is a long and difficult journey back to paradise. It is a pilgrimage, the record of which we have called the history of salvation. That record is written in the still pages of the bible, in the living pages of the liturgy, and in the flesh and blood pages of each man's life.

Recall for a moment something with which you are familar: the ancient biblical pilgrimages. Abraham. He left everything he knew, everything which clung to him and to which he clung. Called and led by God, he journeyed in the desert, following the unseen footsteps of God in the sand. Where was he going? To the land of promise. And there was struggle at every point of the journey, struggle with what we might call the enemy within and the enemy without. Remember Moses and the people of Israel. They, too, left everything they knew—the land of Egypt, which for them was a land of darkness, slavery, death, and that ultimate of evils: sin. Called and led by God, they wandered through endless days and nights in the desert. Headed for the Promised Land, and both fed and led on their way by God, they nonetheless were pursued by everything they left. Liberated from what Egypt represented, they nevertheless constantly longed for what scripture calls the "fleshpots." Their pilgrimage was marked by unremitting struggle, the struggle between the land of promise and the land of exile, the ancient struggle, between good and evil. But the Lord was with them—in the pillar of fire, in food, in water, in forgiveness, in strength: "For the Lord is my shepherd; I shall not want."

Jesus himself was the pilgrim. St. Paul describes his pilgrimage: "Though he was by nature God, (Jesus) did not consider being equal to God a thing to be clung to, but emptied himself, taking the nature of a slave and being made like unto men. And appearing in the form of man he humbled himself, becoming obedient to death, even to death on a cross. Therefore God also has exalted him and has bestowed upon him the name that is above every name, so that at the name of Jesus every knee should bend of those in heaven, on earth and under the earth . . ." (Phil. 2:5-9).

His route led out from the Father across the land of this world and back to the Father. His life was marked with many journeys. You know them as well as I: the flight into Egypt and the return; the pilgrimage from Nazareth to Jerusalem when he was twelve; the forty days in the desert; the continual travel of his public life. And at every point he was pitted against all of the forces of evil which infest men and, indeed, the very world itself. The passage we have read from St. Matthew is but a short example. Jesus' road led to the final struggle recapitulated in the passion, on the cross, and in the tomb. He himself characterized this final stage of the struggle as the hour of the powers of darkness and of the prince of this world. Yet the road led beyond, to resurrection where death and evil itself was swallowed up in victory.

You, too, are on a pilgrimage. You have been called by Christ in his Church, and you have answered with faith-filled commitment. You have followed the lead of the Holy Spirit and presented your minds and hearts as living tablets on which he inscribes the law of love. You have entered into the community of the Church —and the Church has confided to you her belief, the scriptures, her teaching, the creed—her prayer, the Our Father—her faith, the light of the world. The Church has showed you the Lord and you have followed him with steadfast and faithful steps.

This evening marks a milestone in your pilgrimage, for the Church opens up before you another part of the road to baptism: the struggle with evil. The circumstances are most somber and solemn. The prayers and gestures, the questions and answers which we are celebrating this evening are called "exorcism." It is an ancient rite, traceable in its essentials back to the New Testament itself. Conceived from the earliest days as, so to speak, the dark side of baptism, it is filled with images foreign to us: the valley of darkness, the serpent, Satan-Beelzebub, the two kingdoms, the two masters, wrestling against the principalities and powers, the armor of God.

Why this somber solemnity? The Church would have us know two things with absolute clarity. First, evil pursues every man. It followed Abraham. It pursued Moses and the Israelites. It hounded Christ. It harries us: "Our wrestling is not against flesh and blood." And what is this evil? The Gospels present it as the eternal clash between the kingdom of Satan and the kingdom of God: Satan and Christ locked in a cosmic combat for the loyalty and love of man. Sts. John and Paul in the Epistles present it as the "world, the flesh, and the devil."

They do not mean "the world" quite as we would. Rather they mean the world sealed off from God, turned in on itself and on its own resources. That world lives inside each of us and it encircles us. It knows only selfishness, and its resources are dedicated to self. It is a world alien to, and untouched by, genuine love. By "flesh" the apostles do not mean our bodies exactly, but those primordial needs, drives, desires, which, if left ungoverned, conspire to degrade us. They reduce us not to the "human" but to the subhuman. In the figure of the devil or Satan, John and Paul see all those forces—sometimes people—determined to keep us imprisoned in ourselves, in slavery to the flesh, strangers to the love of God and neighbor.

The world, the flesh, and the devil—this is the evil which pursues us, and against which we must struggle with relentless determination. But how can we, simple and weak as we are, have any chance of success? That brings us to the second thing which the Church wants us to know with absolute clarity: we do not struggle alone. Did we not pray together in the psalms: "The Lord is with me; I fear not; what can man do against me? The Lord is with me to help me, and I shall look down on my foes. . . . Give me again the joy of your help, with the spirit of fervor sustain me"? Have we not also read of Jesus who cured the possessed man and cast out the devil? We have just finished reading about the armor of God, the girdle of truth, the breastplate of justice, the shield of faith. And we are just about to pray together: "The Lord is my shepherd, I shall not want. . . . Even though I walk in the dark valley, I fear no evil, for you are at my side."

In a moment or two we will begin the actual exorcism. It is designed to assure you that Christ, who struggled in his own flesh, struggles now in you and with you. He was victorious then—we participate in his victory now. As I trace the sign of the cross over you, your sponsor will mark you on the forehead with the cross. The cross is the sign of Christ's ownership and protection. You are his property and he will fight for you. We, your sponsor and I, and through us, the Church, are your companions and allies. After the signing, I will then pray three times. First I will ask the God of Abraham, Isaac, and Jacob to guard you with vigilant loving-kindness. Then, in the name, in the imitation, and in the power of Christ, I will command the spirit of evil to leave you, and I will seal you with the sign of the cross against his return. Finally, I will pray that the Father will fill your darkness with light.

But none of this is automatic. If the spirit of evil which pursues you and infests you is to leave, and the Holy Spirit is to come, your free consent and cooperation is absolutely indispensable. You will be asked the most ancient questions in the entire liturgy in the Church: "Do you renounce Satan, his works, his enticements?" By your answers you express your free and loving consent to break with evil and to fight steadfastly for the rest of your life. Finally, I will anoint you on the right arm with the sign of the cross. This is to assure you that it is Christ with his whole Church who struggles both in you and at your side.

I have said that this evening is a milestone in your pilgrimage to the promised land of baptism. You re-enact in the liturgy the struggle with evil which will characterize your entire life. It is natural and right to think, "How do I know I will succeed?" There are no guarantees. There is only rugged confidence rooted in the Lord who dwells in the Church. For your struggle is his struggle, the Church's struggle, our struggle. Do not be afraid to fail just as you have not been afraid to go out of yourself on your pilgrimage to the Lord. You take a great risk, but anything to do with love involves a great risk. Should you fall, he, in his infinite mercy, is there to pick you up. Should you get lost in the darkness which infests all of us, the star of his mercy, which can be seen only in the darkness, is there to guide you. Did we not pray together? "Have mercy on me, God in your kindness. In your compassion wipe out my offense. Oh wash me more and more from my guilt and cleanse me from my sin. . . . Oh God, put a steadfast Spirit in me"?

One final word of encouragement. Should you fall after baptism, the central and unseen work of the sacrament of penance is this: to reunite the baptized sinner to Christ in his Church. It is he who acts through the Church to forgive. What happens in the dark confessional is the re-enactment, in mystery, of the poignant encounter between Jesus and the penitent woman.

As St. Luke recounts it, Jesus was dining with Simon the Pharisee. A woman entered the room, bathed the feet of Jesus with her tears, dried them with her hair, kissed them, and then anointed them with ointment. Simon was upset. If Jesus were truly a prophet, would he let such a person even touch him? Knowing what Simon was thinking, Jesus told him of the money lender who had two debtors. One owed 500 pieces of silver and the other, 50. Because neither could pay, he forgave both their debts. When Jesus asked Simon which of the two debtors, in his judgment, would love the money lender more, he answered, " 'He, I suppose, to whom he forgave the more.' " Then Jesus came to the point: " 'Wherefore I say to you, her sins, many as they are, shall be forgiven her, because she has loved much. But he to whom little is forgiven, loves little.' And then he said to her, 'Your sins are forgiven.' And they who were at table with him began to say within themselves, 'Who is this man, who even forgives sins?' But he said to the woman, 'Your faith has saved you; go in peace' " (Lk. 7:47-50). Take courage, then, for he who loves much is forgiven much. Go in peace.

Questions for Discussion

Why should struggle be part of human life?

What advantage does the Christian have in this struggle?

What is the difference between Christian exorcism and black magic?

What reminders do we have of the presence of evil?

Why can the Christian never accept completely the standards of the world?

EIGHTH WEEK: COMMUNION OF SAINTS

DUTIES TO ONE'S NEIGHBOR

Introduction

God made man in such a way that he is dependent in part upon other men for his self-fulfillment.

By birth man becomes part of the human community, and his life will always involve interchange with others.

This social life of mankind implies certain rights and obligations.

Duties and Responsibilities

Everyone has the duty to respect the rights of others.

These rights include principally a right to live, to worship God according to conscience, to hold property, and to enjoy a good reputation.

Over and above these, everyone should have a friendly regard for others and a concern for their welfare.

Hatred, assault, theft, and slander are wrong because they invade these rights and prevent people from growing to personal maturity in the community according to God's design.

Everyone has these rights from the very fact that he is a human being, no matter what his race, religion or color.

We are all travelers on the road, and the successful completion of our common journey calls for mutual help and consideration by all.

The Community

Man has responsibilities to the community as well as to each person in it.

He must fit himself in as best he can and recognize and follow those who are the authentic leaders of the community.

In this and other ways, each person contributes something for the good of the whole.

The community has obligations to each member, too.

It must see that the rights of all are respected and protected.

It must see also that each has what he needs if he is unable to attain this by his own efforts.

The Christian Responsibilities

These rights and obligations apply to all human communities.

The Christian has extra reasons for heeding them.

Christ's command to his disciples was to "love thy neighbor."

So important is this to the Christian that it becomes his identification in the world: "By this shall all men know that you are my disciples—by the love you have for one another."

Sharing the life of God, the Christian shares in his love and concern for all men.

He is the channel through which this love is communicated to men.

The Christian *must* love to be Christian.

Who Is My Neighbor?

These rights and obligations are not abstractions, they are found in people.

Who are these people? Christ told us in the parable of the Good Samaritan.

They are the people whom we actually meet in life—those who are part of our life or merely cross our path.

These are the ones who make our love and concern actual and operative.

Family, friends, fellow workers, neighbors—these have first claim on us; then all the people we don't know: fellow citizens, faraway communities—everyone on the earth is potentially a "neighbor" to everyone else and has a claim on his love and concern.

LITURGICAL ACTION
BIBLE SERVICE

1. An appropriate trinitarian entrance hymn.

2. Prayer for enlightenment.

Priest: O God, come to our assistance.

All: Lord, make haste to help us.

Priest: Glory be to the Father, and to the Son, and to the Holy Spirit,

All: As it was in the beginning, is now, and ever shall be, world without end. Amen.

Priest: The Lord be with you.

All: And with your spirit.

Priest: Let us pray. Lord our God, in times past you visited our father Abraham and made yourself known to your holy people in Israel. Today you are present in the midst of your Body, the Church. Be present this evening as we gather together here for prayer, instruction and discussion. For we have come to know you as Father. We have come to know your only Son, whom you have sent for us and for our salvation. We have come to know your Holy Spirit, who searches the very depths of our hearts. Grant us entry into your inner life. We ask through Jesus Christ, your Son and our Lord.

All: Amen.

3. The people respond to the Word of God:

   a. O Lord, my God, you are great indeed.
   b. You are clothed with majesty and glory,
      robed in light as with a cloak.

   a. You have spread out the heavens like a tent-cloth;
      you have constructed your palace upon the waters.
   b. You make the clouds your chariot;
      you travel on the wings of the wind.

   a. You fixed the earth upon its foundation,
      not to be moved forever.
   b. You water the mountains from your palace;
      the earth is replete with the fruit of your works.

   a. You raise grass for the cattle,
      and vegetation for men's use,
   b. Producing bread from the earth,
      and wine to gladden men's hearts

   a. So that their faces gleam with oil
      and bread fortifies the hearts of men.

b. You made the moon to mark the seasons,
   the sun knows the hour of its setting.

a. You bring darkness and it is night;
   then all the beasts of the forest roam about.
b. The sea also, great and wide,
   in which are schools without number of living things
   both small and great:

a. They all look to you to give them food in due time.
b. When you give it to them, they gather it;
   when you open your hand, they are filled with good things.

a. How manifold are your works, O Lord!
   In wisdom you have wrought them all;
   the earth is full of your creatures.

Priest: Let us pray. God of light and life, you have created visible things in order to lead us to the knowledge of invisible things. Our minds are outstretched for the food of your knowledge. Send forth your Spirit as you have sent forth your Son, so that we may learn to cry "Abba, Father." May we praise you forever.

All: Amen.

4. First reading: 1 Jn. 4:7-16.

5. The people respond to the Word of God:

Priest: Let us kneel and pray. Father Almighty,
All: Give us a share in your strength.
Priest: Creator of heaven and earth,
All: Create us anew in the waters of baptism.
Priest: Father of mercy,
All: Forgive our sins.
Priest: Christ Jesus, born of the Virgin Mary,
All: May we be born again in the font of new life.
Priest: You who were crucified under Pontius Pilate, died and were buried,
All: May we be buried with you in baptism.
Priest: You who were raised from the dead by the Father,
All: May we rise up from the waters of baptism in the newness of life.

Priest: Holy Spirit, who overshadowed the Virgin,
All: Overshadow us with your grace.
Priest: Holy Spirit, advocate and companion.
All: Plead for us always and be with us forever.
Priest: Holy Spirit, teacher and guide,
All: Enlighten our minds and guide our hearts so that we may savor what is true and relish what is right.

6. Second reading: Jn. 14:1-17.

7. Homily.

8. The people respond to the Word of God:

Priest: Let us kneel and pray. God, Father, Son, and Holy Spirit, grant us the grace to offer our whole selves in a sacrifice of love to you.
All: Take, O Lord, and receive all my liberty, my memory, my understanding, and my entire will.
Priest: He who loves me will be loved by my Father, and I will love him and manifest myself to him.
All: Take, O Lord, and receive all that I possess.
Priest: If anyone loves me, he will keep my word, and my Father will love him, and we will come to him and make our abode with him.
All: Lord, you have given me all that I possess. I return it all to you as all I have to give.
Priest: As the Father has loved me, I also have loved you. Abide in my love.
All: Lord dispose my mind and heart and body to be your temple.
Priest: Greater love than this no one has, that one lay down his life for his friends.
All: Lord grant that we may lay down our old lives in the waters of baptism and rise up to walk in the newness of life.
Priest: God, Father, Son, and Holy Spirit, we your family wait anxiously for the baptismal birth of these your well-loved catechumens. Grant them peace of mind, steadfast purpose and generous love. We ask this through Jesus Christ, who suffered and rose for their salvation and for our own. May the blessing of justice and holiness descend upon us all and remain forever.
All: Amen.

9. Recessional: an appropriate trinitarian hymn.

THE TRINITY AND THE CHURCH

God is not the "deity." He is not remote. Quite the reverse. He is intensely present. Remember what Joseph was told: "Do not be afraid, Joseph, son of David, to take Mary your wife, for that which is begotten in her is of the Holy Spirit. And she shall bring forth a son and you shall call him Jesus. . . . Which is interpreted, 'God with us'" (Mt. 1:20-3). These words begin Matthew's Gospel. At the end we read these words of the Lord himself: "All power in heaven and on earth has been given to me. Go, therefore, and make disciples of all nations, baptizing them in the name of the Father, and of the Son, and of the Holy Spirit, teaching them to observe all that I have commanded you; and behold, I am with you all days, even to the consummation of the world" (Mt. 28:18-20). Jesus is the presence of God among men—among us.

God is not an impersonal abstraction. Quite the reverse. Not only is he intensely present, but he is profoundly personal. He is, in fact, three persons. For you have learned to profess: "I believe in God the Father almighty, creator of heaven and earth, and in Jesus Christ, his only Son . . . and in the Holy Spirit" (Apostles Creed). The Father, the Son, and the Holy Spirit are not gods in lonely isolation. Rather they are one God, because they share their deepest selves, their most intimate personal life, with each other in a single life of complete love. "God is love," we have read. This trinity of persons in unity of life is the heart of Christianity. It is not an austere truth proposed for belief, but the central fact of Christian life, made known to us by our Lord and Savior, Jesus Christ, who is the starting point for any genuine knowledge of God.

In the Gospels we see him at great pains—pains which ceased only in the crucifixion—to teach us something so difficult to grasp: in God we have a Father. We have a Father so provident that he feeds even the birds of the air, clothes even the lilies of the field . . . so concerned that he has the very hairs on our heads counted . . . so loving that he sent his only Son for us and for our salvation. "In this is the love, not that we have loved God, but that he has *first* loved us, and sent his *Son* as a propitiation for our sins" (1 Jn. 4:9-11).

Jesus identifies himself as that only Son: "I came forth from the Father and came into the world" (Jn.16:28). So completely is he like his Father that he can say: "He who sees me sees also the Father" (Jn.14:9). St. Paul calls him the brightness of the Father's glory in the image of his substance (Heb.1:3). The Son and his Father are one in mind, one in heart, one in affections—so much so that Jesus says: "I and the Father are one. . . . I am in the Father and he is in me" (Jn. 10:30; 14:11). He is truly the Son of his Father.

Yet the Son came that _his_ Father might be truly _our_ Father. Not only did he teach that in God we have a Father, but that to as many as receive him in faith and in baptism he gives "the power of becoming the sons of God" (Jn. 1:12). He shares with us his own Sonship, so that in him we, too, are true sons of the Father. We are sons in the Son: "I am in my Father and you are in me, and I in you" (Jn. 14:21). Because you are to be sons in the Father's beloved Son, the Church has given you as your heritage both the words and the boldness to say "Our Father who art in heaven . . ."

Perhaps, there is nothing in human life which so besieges us as loneliness; but we must understand above all things that we are not alone, that we are not orphans, that we have not been left to fend for ourselves. Jesus pledges: "I will not leave you orphans" (Jn. 14:18). The Spirit is our teacher who brings to mind whatever the Lord has said: "These things I have spoken to you while yet dwelling with you. But the Advocate, the Holy Spirit, whom the Father will send in my name, he will teach you all things, and bring to your mind whatever I have said to you" (Jn. 14:25-26). He is our companion and guide throughout life: "If you love me, keep my commandments. And I will ask the Father and he will give you another Advocate to dwell with you forever, the Spirit of truth whom the world cannot receive, because it neither sees him nor knows him. But you shall know him, because he will dwell with you, and be in you" (Jn. 14:15-17).

In short, the Holy Spirit is our personal possession. He guarantees that in Christ we are sons and heirs of the Father, for St. Paul writes: "Whoever are led by the Spirit of God, they are the sons of God. Now you have not received the spirit of bondage so as to be again in fear, but you have received a spirit of adoption as sons by virtue of which we cry "Abba! Father!" The Spirit himself gives testimony to our spirit that we are sons of God. But if we are sons, we are heirs also: heirs indeed of God and joint heirs with Christ . . ." (Rom. 8:14-17).

You will become full sons of the Father, joint heirs with Christ, and temples of the Spirit in baptism. In those holy waters each person of the Trinity will establish a most profound personal relationship with each of you individually and all collectively. At that moment the Father becomes fully *your* Father. His beloved Son becomes the *true brother* to each of you, and you become brothers and sisters to each other and to us who have been baptized before you. The Spirit whom the Son sends will be *your* personal guide, elequent advocate, brilliant teacher, and unfailing companion.

But baptism is only the beginning. Each sacrament either establishes or deepens those personal bonds with the Father, Son, and Spirit. In the celebration of each sacrament, we experience and express what the Trinity has accomplished in us. The most privileged place of this experience and expression is the Mass, for there we are gathered together as a family of God, brothers and sisters in Christ. The Son is in our midst: "For where two or three are gathered together for my sake, there am I in the midst of them" (Mt. 18:20). He is present in the scriptures we read there, speaking again those words ever ancient, yet ever new. He is there in the bread and wine to feed us with his body and blood, making present again the Last Supper and Calvary and his resurrection. The Father is there also to receive us as his sons, even if at best we are prodigal sons. And the Holy Spirit is present, opening minds to Christ's words, bringing the bread and wine to life, enriching hearts with courage to follow him wherever he leads.

One final word. The Father, Son, and Holy Spirit will be your full and complete *personal* possession, but not your *private* possession. I have said that the three persons are one God because they share their deepest selves with each other in a single life of complete love. The Church is called to be one in the same sense. Self-giving must characterize life in the Church. For it is to be the sign of the unity of the Trinity, raised high for all men to see—made visible by our sharing ourselves with each other and with all men. Love of neighbor is the proof positive of the Christian. For we read in St. John: "Let us therefore love, because God first loved us. If anyone says, 'I love God,' and hates his brother, he is a liar. For how can he who does not love his brother, whom he sees, love God, whom he does not see? And this commandment we have from him, that he who loves God should love his brother also" (1 Jn. 4:18-21).

At its deepest level, the Church is neither a building nor an institution. It is a community. It is a family whose father is the Father almighty, whose elder brother is Jesus Christ his only Son, whose members are you and I, whose bond of love and solidarity is the Holy Spirit. The Church is the family of God. And when love does not characterize a family, for all practical purposes, it is a family no longer. We members of the Church must give of ourselves to each other: "By this will all men know that you are my disciples, if you have love for one another" (Jn. 13:35). But such love cannot be confined only to our brothers and sisters in the Church. Just as the Father, Son, and Holy Spirit do not keep to themselves, so we must not. If the Father's love has touched the world in his Son to transform it, surely ours should.

The one great Christian commandment is love of neighbor. This is what gives body to the Trinity in the world, our world. And "neighbor" does not mean just loved ones or friends, white men or black men, rich or poor, Christian or Jew. It does not say near or far, stranger or acquaintance. My neighbor is every man, especially a brother or sister human being in need, whether that need is spiritual, emotional, or physical. We members of the family of God are at the service of our fellow human beings in need. For remember: the Father, the Son, and the Holy Spirit are at our service because we are in need. Has not our Lord said: "You call me Master and Lord, and you say well for so I am. If, therefore, I the Lord and Master have washed your feet, you also ought to wash the feet of one another. For I have given you an example, that as I have done to you, so you also should do . . . No servant is greater than his master" (Jn. 13:14-17).

God is intensely present and profoundly personal. He is Trinity in unity, three persons who perfectly share the same life. The Father sent his well-loved Son for us and for our salvation. The Father and the Son send the Spirit to be with us as our constant companion, counselor, teacher, and guide. The Church is the family of the Trinity, the visible embodiment of their life of perfect and complete giving in and to the world. What great dignity is our call and membership in this family. For the strength to heed the call and deepen the membership, let us rise and pray together with boldness and confidence of sons and daughters the prayer taught us by the Savior himself:

"Our Father who art in heaven hallowed be thy name. Thy kingdom come, thy will be done on earth as it is in heaven. Give us this day our daily bread. And forgive us our trespasses as we

forgive those who trespass against us. And lead us not into tempta-
tion, but deliver us from evil. Amen."

Questions for Discussion

What makes God different and so much greater than man?

How can we call God "Our Father"?

What is the Christian's personal relationship with the Holy
Spirit?

Why is the Mass the Christian family get-together?

What is the connection between love of neighbor and life with
God?

NINTH WEEK: THE CHRISTIAN LIFE

PREPARATION FOR EASTER VIGIL

Introduction

The Christian religion is a great action uniting men to God in Christ.

The action began with Christ's coming to earth, and it will end when he returns at the end of time.

Meanwhile it is going on all the time, and Christians live it.

We call it the paschal mystery. All of Christ's actions are now with us in the form of signs, and these signs contain his passage from death to life.

At the Easter Vigil, God's People assemble to rejoice in Christ's victory by celebrating the paschal mysteries and entering ever more deeply into Christ's victory.

At the same time we look forward to their fulfillment at his second coming.

The Easter Vigil service presents these events in words and actions.

Symbols of the Service

A new fire enkindled from flint or rock represents Christ, the fire of God's love, coming forth from the rock of his tomb.

The paschal candle is Christ, the light of the world.

Inscribing Alpha and Omega on it shows Christ to be the beginning and end of everything.

Incense is a symbol of worship; the five pieces in the candle stand for Christ's wounds received in giving himself to his Father.

Lighting the candle symbolizes Christ's coming into a darkened world and spreading his light from person to person through contact with him.

The procession shows the Church following the light of Christ as Israel followed the pillar of fire through the desert to freedom.

This part ends with singing of a song of joy over God's action.

175

Scripture Readings

These describe God's preparations for our redemption in the Old Testament.

The Israelites found God by passing through the Red Sea.

We find him by passing through baptism.

In preparing for baptism we appeal to the Saints for support (litany); those who have already "passed over" these waters.

Blessing of Baptismal Water

Water that will be used in the parish for baptisms during the year is now blessed.

It is breathed on to show that the Holy Spirit will act through it.

The candle is dipped into it, showing that it unites a person to Christ.

Holy oils are poured in to show it is made holy by the Trinity.

Then the baptism itself takes place (review last stage of baptism).

This last step in baptism involves a baptismal font, water and words.

The font symbolizes Christ's tomb: through baptism we die with him to the life of sin and rise to the life of the Spirit.

The water and words symbolize that new life which this action now brings.

Those who have been baptized already participate in this sacrament by publicly renewing the vows of faith and love they made at their baptism.

By this act we express our deliberate commitment to Christ.

The Mass

Then the Easter Mass begins, and we draw together all of the events symbolized in the Vigil service; and they become fully present to us in the eucharist.

Thus in the liturgy of the Church, all of the Christian's life is lived in the actual presence of God's saving actions—past, present, and future.

LITURGICAL ACTION
FOURTH STAGE OF BAPTISM: THE POURING OF WATER

This final step is intended to take place during the Easter Vigil service. The order of that service should be followed except that, in the case of those who have received the first three steps, the ritual begins with the interrogations.

When it is not possible to incorporate this step into the vigil service, the liturgy of the service, including its scripture readings and responses, can be used as the basis for an order of service for this liturgical action.

SUGGESTED HOMILY
THE LIFE OF GRACE

Note: This homily is meant to be given during renewal of baptismal promises. It is addressed to the newly baptized.

Great and world shaking events do not go unremembered. We Americans need only think of the War of Independence which changed the lives of millions, replacing oppression with new hope and security. We recall this event each July 4th with grateful celebration.

Tonight we are all present to take part in the liturgical remembrance and enactment of the world's greatest event—the Easter event of the death and resurrection of Jesus Christ. Here is the center of human history and of Christian belief and hope. We have come as a family of God to give thanks, to relive the meaning of this event and to rededicate ourselves in the renewal of the baptismal promises. And in the midst of all this, we welcome with joy you who are being baptized and received into the Church this evening.

What I want to do is to trace the meaning of the Easter Vigil liturgy. It is part of the instruction to the catechumens being received into our midst and whom I shall address directly. Yet it is meant to help *all* of us appreciate better what tremendous things God has done for us in Jesus Christ.

The overall theme of tonight's liturgy is return from death to life. It is a recurrent theme in the relationship of men with God.

The initial happy relationship of love and friendship which God set up with Adam was rudely destroyed by man's disobedience. Death and slavery to sin came upon the scene. People's lives became ever more self-centered, dominated by pride, conceit, idolatry, immorality.

Still, the loving God was moved to pity and mercy. He set in motion a plan of salvation to reestablish loving contact with men. His first great saving act was to free a tiny, inconspicuous, and enslaved people—the Israelites—from the Egyptians, and make them his very own favored people. It was a two-fold event: freedom from slavery, and new birth as God's people at Mount Sinai.

The liturgy tonight recounts the story of how the Jews, driven by famine to Egypt, eventually ended up terribly oppressed, humiliated, and enslaved. Then God raised up Moses as a great leader who commanded the Pharaoh to let God's people go. But Pharaoh was stubborn; nine plagues failed to move him. The tenth was to be the death of every firstborn in the country. Knowing this would work, Moses told each Israelite family to slay a lamb, eat its flesh, and sprinkle its blood on the doorpost and prepare to leave. Seeing the blood of the lamb, the angel of vengeance passed over and the firstborn of the Israelites were spared. Here is the origin of the Passover or paschal lamb, the sign of Christ, the Lamb of God slain for us.

Well, as soon as the Egyptians let their prisoners go, then Pharaoh changed his mind and sought to recapture them. Just when it seemed as if the Israelities were trapped between the pursuing armies and the Red Sea, the waters opened up to allow them to cross, then closed again to drown the Egyptians. Ever since that time, these saving waters have been a symbol of the saving waters of baptism.

But this escape was only half the story. The passage through the waters was both the low point, when death seemed closest and the beginning of great things. For they were drawn forth and led onto Mount Sinai, where God established them as his people. "I will be your God, and you shall be my people." Scripture describes Israel in the intimate words of son and wife, with God as Father and husband. This new pact or covenant was sealed with the blood of sacrifice. Again it is a symbol of the sacrificial blood of Jesus, which was to seal the new and eternal agreement between God and man. This great saving act of God in favor of the Israelites—bringing them from death to new life—is called the exodus event. It became the very heart and center of the entire Old Testament. Its yearly commemoration in the Passover celebration was not just a remembering, but a belief that the original happenings and particularly their effects were prolonged and made present, so that each new generation might be drawn into the original act which made them God's people.

The death-to-life theme is repeated over and over in the Old Testament, as the people repeatedly sin, fall into idolatry, and are even punished twice by new captivities; yet each time God forgives and restores, and reaffirms his covenant.

Now all these things happening to one nation were only the beginning of what God was about to do for the whole human race, and on a much higher and definitive level. Don't forget, all men were alienated from God, quite hopelessly "on the outs." The original sin of Adam had been confirmed and deepened over and over by man's own personal sins.

What is sin? Well, it is not so much a black mark against us as a shattered relationship. So redemption was not so much a debt to pay as a bridge to cross, a relationship to restore. It was hardly something that weak, irresolute, self-centered men could do by themselves—any more than the Israelites could have brought about the exodus event all by themselves! So God once more put his plan of salvation into action, this time in a once-for-all and final way. He sent his own Son in the form of man to rebuild the bridge from man back to God. Without ceasing to be God, Jesus hid his divine qualities, and as St. Paul says "emptied himself, taking the nature of a slave." Scripture portrays him as the new Moses who was to lead the world back to God, and as the sacrificial Lamb in whose blood we are saved.

In his human nature Jesus was exactly as we—with the same emotions and inclinations, the same temptations to self-centered way of living. But he overcame all this. "He humbled himself, becoming obedient unto death, even the death on the cross." Loving-obedience was the key. By this he reversed the process of man moving away from God. He willingly surrendered all he had —even that which men hold most dear, life itself.

But death on the cross was only half the story. Acceptance of an offering is all important. The resurrection and glorification of Jesus is the Father's acceptance. Jesus receives not just the old life of the body back again, but is inundated with the life of the Spirit, which gives all the new and glorious qualities to his risen body. In fact his risen humanity now becomes the source of this same divine life for all his followers. Jesus' death and the Father's acceptance by which Jesus is raised up again in glory to the right hand of the Father is the definitive death-life theme of the Easter liturgy.

Now we can see where baptism fits in. The early Christians were vividly aware that baptism was the insertion of each Christian into this great saving event of Christ's death and resurrection. Where better to place it but on Holy Saturday in the Easter vigil liturgy. You remember hearing, I'm sure, how baptisms used to take place in rather large pools. The catechumen went down into the water—symbol of dying with Christ—and arose to newness of Christ's risen life. Today's simplified version tends to emphasize the washing away of sin—which is all right; but we should remember the symbolism of the Red Sea and of dying and rising with Jesus. St. Paul puts it nicely: "Do you not know that all we who have been baptized into Christ Jesus have been baptized into his death? For we were buried with him by means of baptism into death, in order that, just as Christ has arisen from the dead through the glory of the Father, so we also may walk in newness of life" (Rom. 6:3-5). We are even said to be "inserted into Christ," so that, as Paul says, "I live, now no longer I, but Christ lives in me."

One who receives baptism is immediately and deeply changed. We are no longer mere creatures and servants, but adopted sons and daughters of the Father, with Christ as our brother. The difference is grace. Grace means first of all the totally undeserved graciousness and mercy of God by which he saves us because of Jesus. Secondly, it means the new life given us so that we can respond with true faith and love to God's offer of friendship. Grace, then, should never be thought of as some kind of "electric current" or "thing" which flows through sacramental pipelines. Rather, it is *life,* the same life of the Spirit that made Jesus so pleasing to the Father in heaven. God cannot give grace from a million miles away. He gives it by giving himself, as if interiorly and continously imprinting on us from within something of his own trinitarian life.

Valid baptism can be given only once, and we Catholics must be ready to acknowledge that wherever it is given, it is a once-for-all insertion into Christ. This is why some of you may only be taking part in the profession of faith. Again, we Catholics do not pretend that God withholds all grace from adults who haven't had a chance for baptism. The sincere but unbaptized adult may often receive God's grace to respond to whatever concept of God he is able to have; he may well be an "anonymous Christian." But even if you have already received grace, and were somehow related to the Church, your baptism or profession of faith is very important. It fills out your initiation into the worshiping family of God, it puts you into full communion with the people of God, it incorporates you fully into Christ. Just as the Israelites were a single and visible people made holy by their election and called to give united worship to their God, even more are we called to open, joyful, and common worship and praise.

The Easter Vigil liturgy is the most exciting of the whole year. And like all liturgy it is far more than a memorial service; there is a real presence of Christ and his saving power. Just as the Israelites believed that the yearly Passover service mysteriously made present the events of the exodus, so we Christians believe even more that the saving events of Christ's death and resurrection are made present—that they mysteriously leap over space and time to be effective among us this evening. All the more reason for fervent and personal response in everything that takes place here tonight—whether it be your baptism or profession of faith, or our renewal of baptismal promises.

There is a scarcely restrained note of joy in the Easter liturgy, particularly in the Mass that follows. Just listen to the bells at the "Glory to God" or the repeated "alleluias." This is because the long centuries of waiting came to an end in Christ. With him is inaugurated the "final era," the era bathed in the grace and redemption of Jesus, who now stands as our Savior and risen Lord, as first-born from the dead (Col. 1:18) and the pledge of our salvation. "Unless Christ be raised up our faith is in vain," says St. Paul. But Christ has been raised up and glorified. He is the living proof of the Father's mercy and grace toward us. We have made a basic acceptance in baptism. For all of us, this commitment must grow and increase. Only in proportion as we lay aside our own whims, self-interests and self-centeredness can the grace and life of Christ Jesus transform us and bring to perfection the new birth in us. Through the liturgy and the sacraments we are resurrected bit by bit until that final self-emptying in Christian death which makes room for the total transformation into the risen life of Jesus.

No longer are you catechumens. You are now full-fledged members in our Christian family here. Joyfully we welcome you on this night of splendor and rejoicing. Let us help each other realize what it means to be a true witness to our risen Lord, and show by our lives that we really take him seriously as our Way and our Truth and our Life.

THE POST-CATECHUMENATE

Although no material is offered here for a post-catechumenate, the importance of some kind of follow-up program is such that it deserves at least a mention.

When a catechumen is finally received into the Church this does not mark the end of catechesis. It really means a new beginning— the launching out of a full fledged member of the Church on his lifelong task of growth in Christ. Part of the Church's pastoral mission is to supply him with the spiritual riches that will make this possible. The needs of new Catholics are special and continuing education in the faith is a principal one. Hence, any effective post-catechumenate program should amply provide further study of scripture and of the spirituality and doctrinal teaching of the Church. No special format is necessary, but the content should aim at covering once again the main elements of Catholic faith.

Few parishes have had such a post-catechumenate in the past. However, this is changing. The developments of Vatican II and the consequent pastoral necessity to re-form the minds and hearts of Catholics have called forth new attempts to establish adult catechetical programs. Where these exist and center on the great documents of Vatican II, a ready-made post-catechumenate is at hand. There is no necessity in such circumstances to set up a special program for new Catholics. They can join their older brethren in the common Christian effort to put on the mind of the Church which is none other than the mind and heart of Christ.